THIS BOOK IS DEDICATED TO

GISELA KONOPKA AND MARLA RUZICKA

Neither of these women waited for support from "the system" or inspiration from "the culture" around them. Both focused on getting some merciful outcome for people oppressed by huge organizations.

Gisela was a resistance fighter during World War II. She escaped from a concentration camp and reached the United States in 1941. She founded the University of Minnesota's Center for Youth Development.
Gisa died in Minneapolis in 2003 at age 93.

Marla Ruzicka was only 23 years old when she went door to door to assess the suffering of Iraqi citizens from American invasion. She founded the Campaign for Innocent Victims in Conflict and secured millions of dollars in aid money from the United States federal government for distribution in Iraq.
Marla was killed by a car bomb on April 16th, 2005. She was 28 years old.

# Table of Contents

| | |
|---|---:|
| Dedication of This Book | 5 |
| Our Shout—in Brief | 9 |
| A Shout to American Clergy | 11 |
| Three Psychological Dynamics to Think of: | 17 |
|    1. Leadership as a *psychological dynamic* remarkably different from followership | 17 |
|    2. *Holy* and *moral* language as *psychological dynamics* remarkably different from business language | 28 |
|    3. Courage to do something *alone*, with God or without God, as a *psychological dynamic* remarkably different from leading one's ministry | 36 |
| An Empathy-Based Stage-Development Theory | 45 |
| The Appendix with its Table of Contents | 81 |
| The Index | 97 |

# Our shout—in brief

Dear ordained clergyperson:

This is our request to you: that you as a private citizen focus on saving the American judicial system.

Please do not check in with your Vestry or church council. Do not seek "support," with all that means, from your laity. Don't rope them in no matter how wonderfully they may volunteer.

Do not rope lay ministers into this particular project even if they are willing.

Let your congregation or the activists among them start up or continue the usual projects that moral, civic activists tend to do. They will be hopping onto buses to demonstrate on the Mall. They will be signing letters. They will and do courageously pay for advertisements in huge newspapers that consist largely of columns of names of people afraid of losing a judiciary system that cares for American rights. Followers and young people will have vigils on overpass bridges and on street corners. Let them. Those projects are great, and followers can jolly each other up to carry them off. There's nothing wrong with them.

What we are asking *you* to do, however, is alone to contact members of the Senate by e-mail and telephone and ordinary mail and in person. Ask them to save the American judiciary system.

This, like any project that leaders, as opposed to followers, are up for will show your head above the crowd. No one will attack or even harass a busload full of likeminded citizenry or rough up a crowd of idealists in the National Mall looping around with their signs.

If, however, you few talk to Senators using passionate language instead of the usual non-profit-organization language, or the corporate gas that we all know how to talk, you will be heard in an uncommon way. Who talks about deliberately endangering the judicial system as "cruel?" Who *should* refer to it as *cruel* or as not *cruel*? It is a question of whether you think of yourself as someone "concerned" or as someone "outraged" when government is cruel. Of all the people in helping, or at least non-hurting, professions you clergy people likely distinguish best between appreciatively touching a museum suit of armor and putting the whole thing on. Or the difference between blog and prayer.

— Carol Bly and Cynthia Loveland

# A Shout to American Clergy

This is a proposal to few, not thousands.

It is a request from laypeople to men and women who are official, ordained heads of churches. Please use your taste for moral life to help save the United States judicial system.

We feel sure that the psychological effect of your private efforts, provided you use the language of religious passion, will be a surprise to the United States Senate.

Nearly everyone who takes pains to write Senators at all starts the e-letter or ordinary letter by bleating, then second, warms to the task—look! Here I am writing a letter to a Senator!—and third, billows into the most boring pomposity. We noticed how people writing even to outspoken moralists like Senator Byrd would repeat back to him, but in gassy language, his own ideas. That's the usual thing. What if that Senator or anyone else, say, Winston Churchill, had gone on and on about finding the destruction of rights and freedom "counter-productive" or "matters of concern?"

Rationale for this plea—

Our Constitution stipulates three branches of government: the Executive, or President, the Legislative—or House and Senate of the Congress, and the Judicial—or Supreme and other courts. The idea is that no one branch, and thus no one party, even when in power, may control everything.

Today, with like-minded extremists in control of both the executive and legislative branches, the Judiciary is the hope remaining for keeping a balance of power. With more and more serious attempts by the majority in power to also control and undermine the judiciary it is crucial to prevent this from happening.

Federal Judges and Supreme Court Justices are appointed for life. Thus their decisions have incrementally longer impact than decisions made by either the President or the Congress. And because the justices are appointed, with advice and consent of the Senate, not elected, citizens have no part in choosing. The nearest citizens get to choosing judges is to have had the good sense or luck to have elected wise and disinterested[1] Senators. Whenever the Supreme Court, for example, decides to interpret the Constitution in some manner by which it can nullify previous laws by declaring them unconstitutional, such decisions dismantle one or another part of our built-up infrastructure.

Destroyed structures of justice and law are horribly difficult to rebuild.

For starters, the Constitution is easily compromised without many Americans' knowing it. More and more young people graduate from high school without knowing much American history: tens of thousands of them haven't the least idea what is meant by "separation of church and state." They don't feel nervous about issues like vouchers to pay private schools out of public-school funds. They don't feel nervous about it for the same reason that they are not nervous about covert shipping or not shipping political prisoners to foreign countries known for torturing inmates. They would have no way of knowing how often in the past the Supreme Court has been a threat, or a blessing, as the case might be.

It is a waste of time to try to rouse people to action who have never heard of a painful truth such as how vulnerable, actually, the Congress is when the Supreme Court wields too much power. Hearing and believing, never mind acting upon, *painful information* is not a strength of followers. Say that we try to explain to someone who knows scarcely any U.S. history how Thomas Jefferson was downhearted all the last 17 years of his life because the Supreme Court snatched freedoms away from the republic that he had worked for.[2] The response of a citizen who both knew no history and was brought up in group-

---

[1] We use the word "disinterested" in its classic courtroom meaning: *"not being compromised by financial benefits to oneself."*
[2] For a description of how the Supreme Court came by its power to adjudge Congressional legislation already made and signed by the President, see a description of Marbury v Madison, 1804, in the Appendix.

schmooze would be to say that, whoever that old person was with the weird depression they should get a grip. An uninformed citizen not only doesn't know desperately sad information but instinctively will reject it when it's offered. Katherine Ann Porter's *Ship of Fools*—both excellent book and excellent movie—had two memorable bon mots. Her ship of fools was a passenger ship en route to Bremen, just before World War II. After dinner one evening, the omnipresent German band started playing German street music. A man turned to the little person next to him and said, "Ah, when you hear such German music, doesn't it give you a very special feeling about being a German?" to which the little man said: "When I hear music like that, it gives me a very special feeling about being a dwarf." In another conversation a Jew at the captain's table said, in response to some non-German's discussion of Jews being in big trouble in the New Germany, "Well, but they can't kill us all, can they?" Porter's main genius as a writer of American literature was her constant pointing, directly or not, to injustices lying just beneath the surface of life.

Whenever the Supreme Court crouches hugely over the Congress, the issue is not always clear. In our time, President Bush and rightist-thinking people want an imperially-inclined Supreme Court to weaken the rights of the common people. Here, however, is another view of a President's maneuvering with the Supreme Court: Abraham Lincoln harshly shook the "balance of powers" in order to save the United States itself. He regarded a saved Union as the lesser of two evils, so he reached out for this heavy tool, the Supreme Court, and swung hard. This is why Constitutional history makes uneasy reading. As Robert George said recently "Unchecked power to do good is unchecked power to do evil."[3]

Here is how this would work now. Say that many of the 900 federal judgeships and the Supreme Court were filled with right-wing extremists. It would not matter whom we elected as

---

[3] Robert George, professor of jurisprudence and director of the James Madison Program in American Ideals and Institutions at Princton, speaking at dinner to the Hoover Institution, October 27, 2003, on "Judicial Supremacy? Lessons from Lincoln."

President or legislators during the next 40 years because those presidents and Congresspeople would find that whatever humane and peace-respecting legislation they initiated or signed, if it involved constraint on the greed of the rich in power, would be nullified as unconstitutional by the Supreme Court. Extremists' goals are neither humane nor respectful of peace: they are the goals of empire.

Psychologically speaking, what are the goals of an emperor? Here are four. They are not logical components of human thinking—they are not entities studied in advanced schools of political science or even at War Colleges.[4] They are essentially *psychological*.

1. Fun—

Fun is an under-recognized pleasure of emperors. One kind of fun is bullying people now and then because you can, with impunity. Senator Byrd tells the story of the Roman emperor who was accosted in public by a Senator who accused him of unfairness to the ordinary people. The emperor smiled and said, "You are behaving appropriately for a Senator—bringing this to my attention. Now I am going to behave appropriately for an emperor." He called up a guard and told him to cut off the Senator's head. The guard did so. Lesser, but with the same curious fun-seeking in it: Senator Jesse Helms whistled Dixie when Carol Moseley Braun stepped into the elevator he was in. Senator Braun, a black woman, had licked a Helms bill in 1993 for renewing a patent for an insignia of the Confederate Battle Flag for the United Daughters of the Confederacy. Helms, talking about the elevator incident, blithely granted that he really just wanted to see if he could make her cry.

---

[4] One of the most well-known texts given first-year cadets in military academies is Carl von Clausewitz's *On War*. For over a century it was condemned by Prussian military officers because it gives serious weight to psychological factors in war-making. Clausewitz was an easy put-down, having been an enlisted man who only later was made an officer. He had a very interesting idea, a lot like Machiavelli's thinking but more specific, and shrewder and less beastly than Sun Tzu's. Clausewitz had the prescient notion that if you empathize with others you will be exercising those parts of the imagination that enable you better to guess what those others might do next.

2. Self-interest—
Less tax paying for one's friends and less government money spent in schools, public health, and other services to the hoi polloi.

3. Hobby wars—
Perhaps because the editorial staff of Bly & Loveland Press are women we don't seem to have any grasp of why a person would want to start a hobby war. For power, yes, of course, but that is too vague and too partial an answer. Perhaps the pleasure in being able to order hundreds of 18-year-olds to suit up for likely death or dismemberment is a gender-specific evil. In general, however, our publishing house tends not to respect the idea of gender-specific evils, or virtues either. Condoleezza Rice comes to mind on the one hand and John the Baptist on the other.

Wars started by middle- and old-aged males for pleasure may be a subject we should pay more attention to than we have done. Stephen Spender and Robert Graves and Siegfried Sassoon have given us major literature precisely on this subject—old men cottoning to sending youth off to wars. The psychologist James Hillman has recently written about it under the title *A Terrible Love of War*.[5] Barbara Tuchman made horrifying side-swipes at the hobby war mentality in *The Guns of August*.[6]

History is full of big-name leaders addicted to hobby-warring. Some of them had even had excellent, principled teachers in their adolescence. One with minimal self-control was Alcibiades of Athens in its post-democratic period. Alcibiades was educated in the ancient Greek equivalent of Deerfield and Princeton. He had been a student and admirer of Socrates. As an adult he was so charismatic the people would cheer for him although most of his exertions were anti-democratic and his military projects uselessly destroyed Greek soldiery. He would campaign now for one cause, now for another, some of it for material gain, some for psychological fun. Although he himself didn't participate in

---
[5] James Hillman, *A Terrible Love of War*. New York: Penguin, 2004. Hillman is a Yale professor and author of many books and a leader in much contemporary Jungian thought.
[6] Tuchman, Barbara W., *The Guns of August*. New York: Macmillian Publishing Company, 1988.

the campaign, he was the main instigation for the attack on Sicily that basically finished off the Athenian empire. It was a disaster. Most of the foot soldiers whom the Navy took to Sicily never came home. They died of wounds and in swamps and thousands were taken prisoner. What is interesting about Alcibiades was his puerile dislike of any constraint. He seems to have had just the combination of privilege and vanity to inspire projects that were generally very bad news for those common people who got drafted to them.

A key fact: fifth-century Athens couldn't check dangerous leaders the way an adverse American Congress can, or the way a disinterested Supreme Court can check a President who keeps pressing to get his way.

4. Power for oneself and one's friends, for the enjoyment of it—

A classical psychological goal of emperors is to take as much power away from people as you can and distribute it, often with beneficient panache, among your friends.

Specifically, what powers of people would be taken away if our Republic should be shredded back to empire?[7]

>    Civil rights
>    Freedom of speech
>    Freedom of the press
>    Freedom of public assemblage
>    Fairness on economic issues
>    Separation of church and state

Hence our request that you clergy, alone or in twos, quickly get in touch with Senators, keeping your focus on the judiciary system.

---

[7] We say shredded "back" to empire because a few leaders' bullying a population of followers is Nature's plan. It's the retro government style of wolves, ants, and all mammals and insects in between. The idea of a Republic is not natural. It is an ingenious, ethical invention of homo sapiens's thalamocortical reentry. That is why Wendell Phillips, anti-slavery man, speaker, and columnist, told the Massachusetts Anti-Slavery Society in 1852 that "Eternal vigilance is the price of liberty." You get empire easily enough without any vigilance. All you need is for "good people to do nothing."

Qualities clergy people will need for this project:
1. Leadership as in *going it alone*, taking no committee with you.
2. The use of the two least popular kinds of language:
    a. Holy language and
    b. Abstract language.
3. Courage. Both personal courage and professional risk-taking

## Part 1. Leadership as a *psychological* dynamic

Leaders are people who act alone either because the job requires working alone or because they have vision ahead of their time. Spying has to be done alone. Writing poetry must be done alone to be any good.[8] Mathematics has to be done alone. Prayer has to be done alone when it is a conversation with God, as opposed to liturgical acting, ironically enough sometimes called "corporate prayer."

An unromantic reason for people of vision to do their work alone is that news from them isn't likely to be greeted cordially. Anyone who has gone to a respectable seminary knows what the crowd was like around people like Boethius and St. Philip of Heraklea. An ordinary clergyperson may as well do as much of his or her envisioning alone simply to avoid being excoriated by fools.

Most of what American clergy attend to is administrative direction, not leadership. Administration must be done well, too. Clergy should be facilitators in a good many disheartening discussions without showing a glimmer of boredom or scorn. This work is exhausting, but one can also be a *leader* at least in these two ways: first, keep telling your parishes about the sobering *complexity* of Christianity and of Judaism. Most clergy do do that,

---

[8] Doing arts or mental work in groups is so much in vogue now, however, that Mary Oliver's and William Wordsworth's straightforward statements to the contrary—that literature can't be written in groups—far from inhibits the American creative-writing industry. The half-century-old Harkness pedagogy of Phillips Exeter Academy—putting young people around oval tables so they can trade opinions and impressions as they "discuss" in their classrooms—has a death-cool grip on high-school teaching. Americans are always in groups. One has to be alone to be in possession of one's own take on things, but Americans are nearly never alone. It's especially important for clergy people to think about Americans' being so seldom alone.

because they went to the pulpit in the first place with a gratitude for what theology gives us. So they try to explain such profound ideas as *atonement*. It is hard to explain directly to a congregation full of conservative-minded people that if they clipped someone at their workplace—let us say, they took departmental instruction from high up that said shave the workers' overtime hours because the firm doesn't want to pay out that much—let us say they did that—how do you tell them to figure out how much they clipped each given worker in their department and *start paying it back?* Most preachers tell their people that someone else atoned for their sins already. That remark allows conservatives and idealists to sit next to each other in the pews.

Whatever your solution to doctrinal problems you can do private projects like writing and talking to the Senate about justice in addition. Your success will depend upon whether you can make yourself use religious, compassionate language instead of management language. If you have been using follower, that is, management language for a number of years it will be awfully hard to use leadership language. Think of it this way: follower language is extroverted and leadership language is from inner feeling. For a woman, let's say, who all her life has done only practical tasks, it is hard to use passionate language. A priest or pastor or rabbi who has learnt to schmooze[9] in seminary discussions may find it hard to use passionate language.

If we try to think through the general differences between the *feeling* life of the cleric and the *feeling* life of most communicants a question comes up almost immediately: in 2005, what are the *feelings* that make people go to church anyhow?

---

[9] Schmooze language is made of evasive, cordial word choices. Different classes and age groups of people schmooze differently. Teenagers, for example, when asked for an opinion can and do schmooze out of it with "Well, I'm like, hello?" or "I'm like, hey, am I missing something here?" The best schmooze I ever heard was from a Protestant pastor who was told by a Bible Study participant that "Paul told the Galatians that God makes us sick for a punishment." The point of Galatians is that God does *not* make anyone sick for punishment but this pastor was an adroit schmoozer. He said, "Yes, yes, that is one of the things Paul said. But he also said that we can trust God not to make us sick as a punishment." A serious schmoozer like that can tell you that it is beginning to rain and now at last the sun is coming out in the same breath and then add in a sage and fully friendly tone, "But of course we must take things in their context."

1. If lay members of churches practice any imaginative activism they do not expect, as Nathan Hale did, to be hanged for it if it goes wrong. Clergy and lay people whose activism takes the form of getting on buses and herding to Washington to do 1970s-style demos in the Mall also do not expect to be imprisoned or even just harassed by the IRS or any other federal agency .
2. Congregations by and large are not much interested in religious passion. They have a remarkable enjoyment of clerical hobby-work instead. When I attended the C of E in England a couple there fed bats behind the reredos. Any church built of Essex rubble stone in the 14$^{th}$ century has bats. This couple put out plates of feed and water for them. Only the flower rota people, who also stored vases back there, were annoyed by the bat food or bat droppings. Neither the bat-prep couple nor the flower rota whom I knew nor the women who did off the brasses showed interest in what was said from the pulpit or from the Scripture-reading lectern. Still, all of them attended church for both Mass and Evensong and contributed their labor without cease. They were C of E life-stylists. I don't think their vicar, Fr. Jack Putterill, could have talked them into any single opinion of Jesus's that he admired.
3. Educated couples raising children in America have to decide which is the lesser of two evils: bringing up their children to some doctrines they themselves swear to each Sunday but are lying about, or not bringing their children to any church. In the one case they practice, model, and thus *normalize* lying. In the second, they deprive the children of ever hearing abstract, principled language about love and mercy and justice. Children who don't get into churches hear very little praise of invisible qualities of life. They may easily fail to develop a taste for praising virtue as such.
4. Members of loyal congregations tend to allow themselves a lot of satisfying we/they thinking. They regard themselves as your reliable cadre. They feel that you are lucky to have them. [And so you are. It would be grim to face a nave full of

meth makers and dealers every Sunday.] Congregations fairly bask in the good opinion of fellow-worshippers. Constantly poulticing themselves, as they tend to, with such self-congratulation, however, nurtures some absent-mindedness at U.S.A. election times. Why would that be? Just as absolute power corrupts absolutely, self-congratulation absolutely immunizes the self-congratulator from even noticing difficult ideas, never mind recognizing crises. Self-congratulation keeps a person from asking, "Listen, Father (Pastor, Rabbi), if there is wickedness out there, what exactly should we be doing?"

5. When the parish is a rural parish its members are especially at risk to allow themselves too much self-congratulation. Clearly some of their members should become leaders. Stage-development philosophy[10] shows us how human beings can gradually widen the circle of others whom they can tolerate or even feel some empathy for. No adult should be left still stuck in stages 2, 3, or 4 if there is any chance that mentoring or a dollop of liberal-arts education or psychotherapy might wake their minds to stage 5 life—the life of someone who stands on his or her own conscience.

6. A surprising psychological dynamic is this: congregations often allow themselves to be do-nothings even in crises because to followers *fearfulness* is all right. You are smart, followers usually think, to act upon fearfulness. If Nathan Hale was sorry he had but one neck to stick out, most church populations don't share the feeling. Thomas Hardy cannily remarked in his journal of October 17, 1896, that "if Galileo had said the earth moved in *verse* the Inquisition would have left him alone." Young poets publish books of verse against President Bush's wars. They are safe enough. For someone like the President and his crowd killing a poet would be like getting caught tromping on a baby robin. Emperors and presidents and cops are always convinced that poetry is moral fluff. Emperors don't care what criticism they get in

---

[10] See page 45 An Empathy-based stage-development theory.

any literary format. They are not psychologically stupid by any means. An example from long ago is the great satirist Aristophanes who, we are taught, was wonderfully outspoken against this or that rotten governing program, especially wonderfully outspoken against Cleon, whom he despised. You would think Cleon would send around some toughs and gather in Aristophanes, and thus cow other playwrights. But no. Aristophanes's play, "The Knights," was an unsurpassed success when performed. It won first prize by acclamation. People laughed and shouted the ancient Greek equivalents of Way to go! And That's telling 'em!  The audience hooted not just at Aristophanes's formidable sex jokes, but at his accurate satire of Cleon's politics. Then everybody went home and that was the end of it. Cleon knew perfectly well that artists, if you leave them be, split themselves in two anyway: they handsomely write a lot of bravado and strong morals and damning of cruel policies, using a lot of real names of living politicians, but then they go home and put their laurel leaves in water. In his first play, Aristophanes had "painted the miseries of war and invasion arising from [Cleon's] mistaken and mischievous line of action, and had dwelt on the urgent necessity of peace in the interests of an exhausted country and ruined agriculture."[11] Who cared? No one.

It is a widely-made but serious mistake in judgment to think only top-ranking soldiers split themselves into their theoretical beliefs and their comfortable private lives. The psychiatrist Robert Jay Lifton wrote most feelingly about this as it showed in Nazis. Lifton called it "doubling." His book about it makes good reading—good, but unpleasant reading— in the way that someone's memoir makes good reading when the memoirist describes some repellent behaviors that you have practiced in your *own* life.[12]

---

[11] From the unidentified translator's Preface to *Five Plays of Aristophanes*.
[12] Robert Jay Lifton and Erik Marcussen, *The Genocidal Mentality*, New York: Basic Books, 1990.

A half-hidden truth is that one can be a follower by practicing something that looks wonderfully activist but in fact that doesn't offend any too-large enemies. At the time of this writing church laity, laced with clergy, plan to spend around $100,000 busing themselves to Washington.[13] There is not a chance in the world that Homeland Security would commit any cruelty against such an attractive and upper-middle-class mob. Besides, if everyone who took exception to the Bush Administration's injustices just got on buses with loud-speakers, that would draw off the fire of serious dissenters like Bob Herbert and Maureen Dowd and Bill Moyers. It is true that Christians teach one another that Jesus

> Knew (he was going to be crucified if he didn't back down)
> Wept. ("Father, if it be thy will, take this cup from me.")
> Then went anyway—
> Therefore, fear not!

"So what?" is the average church-attender's take on that. Jesus modeled extraordinary courage. But it doesn't shame present-day churchgoers out of their own fearfulness because Jesus is said to be part of a triune God. A *God*. That lets us off the hook. Just because a God was up for knowing terror of his own death but making a dangerous stand anyhow—that doesn't mean *we* have to. Besides, that was *then*, and this is *now*.

Speaking of that very popular phrase, "That was then, this is now:" it is one of two phrases dear to followers. The other one is "You have to put things into their context." We would all be in bad shape if the Buddha or Moses or Jesus had decided to put anything into any context. If you look analytically at those two phrases—*That was then: this is now* and *You have to put things in context*—you see that both deny eternal truths. Both encourage

---

[13] Clergy and Laity Concerned About Iraq have begun organizing a national bus tour for which an estimated $100,000 is wanted. A brisk, handsome website for information is http://www.clnnlc.org. Other organizations in which one does not endanger oneself or one's family include the National Foundation of Churches, Church Folks for a Better America, National Council of Churches, and Bread for the World.

what is called cultural relativism—that is, each historical happening has no particular meaning except to those who were there. Those two statements undercut any universal abstract truth one might draw from an occasion. Only science and liberal-arts educations, especially math, support a love of universal truths. If one hears nothing all one's life but individual anecdotes which amount to nothing but a drifting tourism past some psychological landmarks, then one acquires no taste for universals—for the All Things Invisible that churchgoers profess themselves thankful for.

You can beautifully see the difference between some people's love of universals and other people's love of specific occasion for its own sake if you visit a retirement home and listen to the conversations. Anecdote, anecdote, anecdotes going past one another without passionate listeners enough to go around.

Christianity, like other passionate and complex religions, is probably too much for most of us. We are followers. And we want to be followers. We are sheep in wolves' clothing.

All this in order to emphasize how very different a pastor's or priest's or rabbi's own philosophy should be from follower-philosophies!

The problem of psychological drift—

Social workers make a distinction in their work environments between *primary* and *secondary settings.*

A primary setting is typically an agency staffed by a majority of social workers. In such a setting the young or less experienced worker is surrounded by colleagues who can lend support and consultation. The atmosphere is infused with the principles and attitudes of the young person's own profession.

A secondary setting is an environment in which the social worker is alone, collaborating on demanding tasks with people of other professions. A school, a hospital, a medical clinic, or a nursing home is a secondary setting for its social workers.

In general it is better for young social workers to have their first experience in a primary setting than in a secondary setting, because the principles, goals, and perspectives of those around them will be those of their own profession. Each day's work with colleagues in a primary setting models and mentors the young worker in his or her own professional identity.

We mention this because clergy are almost always tossed from Seminary into a church and the church is a secondary setting. That makes that young clergyman or clergywoman the lone person of their own profession in their workplace.

One aspect of the clergy's *loneness* in the congregation is that he or she is so often pressured away from clean-cut feeling about things theological or moral, either one or both. After all, most congregational affairs are laypeople's issues. Even if the issues are questions of morality, and laypeople are glad to have a pastor at the meeting, the laypeople still feel "entitled to their opinion," as the expression goes. Sometimes you see whole U-shaped tables set up in a parish hall, filled with some regional or local lay leaders who are worrying some problem. They want the clergyperson to open that meeting with prayer, then stay out of it for at least 10 minutes, then when asked for the right solution to provide the solution the laity agree on, and then to close the meeting with prayer.

Irving Janis, in his great book *Groupthink*, identified "moral drift."[14] Moral drift is a group phenomenon. Let us say that you, a cleric, enter the group meeting feeling strongly in favor of Program A. The others prefer Program B. What's more, the others are relaxed about it. They are looking around at one another just as much as they are looking at you. They seem to say. "We all kind of like B, don't we?" Their tone says. "What's the fuss? Let's have more light and less heat in here." Program A, which you had rather loved and hoped for, is not even getting further mention in the group's conversation. No one is wildly opposed. They simply are not interested.

---

[14] Janis, Irving, *Groupthink*. 1983. Boston: Houghton Mifflin Company.

It is hard to be the only person who cares for Program A at all, but no clergy person should get shrill. Shrill, as any 1990s facilitator of corporate ethics meetings can tell you, is death. It is anti-schmooze. You are experiencing Moral Drift if their B-liking and their laid-backness have soaked through and stained your belief in Program A.

In this book we use the expression *psychological drift* for what all parish clergy are faced with. We see it this way: moral drift happens on a single given occasion when the group is mild-tempered and laid-back and not much interested in the issues. One individual (perhaps you, the pastor) came into the room resolved to waken that group to some adherence to a certain principle. Gradually, as the afternoon wears on, you have given it up. The others feel that you have given it up. People now smile, now that you've taken the middle position—you are neither for nor against Program A or B, and when asked to wrap up you say that A and B each has something really wonderfully valuable to give us. They now feel easy. They wait for your closing prayer.

That's one occasion. Psychological drift, as opposed to moral drift, is upon you when a year has passed and you have capitulated to moral drift so many times you cannot quite recall ever having been so rampant on some subject or other! You look back on the year and tell yourself, "How did I get so worked up? Those people, I have to say, have been wonderfully patient with me!" *That* is psychological drift. It is long-term.

We postulated six psychological aspects of congregations.

Here are a few of the psychological aspects of a religious leader, if he or she really is a leader at all.

This leader has a career commitment to what he or she sees as leadership work for God. This commitment might be only the commitment of a skilled administrator, but at least you are following a career in which you on top don't have to be paid 100 times the average workers' pay of the whole organization lest you quit for lack of "executive compensation."[15] By definition, because you are a clergy person, you are above the regular run of corporate avarice. You are a principled person.

In the case of Christians and Jews, your intellectual training especially honors the individual person's break with casual, languorous human society. Moses and Jesus are the heroes, not the groupies of self-interested Jews and self-interested Christians. In political things, Patrick Henry and Nathan Hale (the first who shouts alone, the second willing to spy alone) were leaders who did work alone or, to use the Social Work expression, worked in *very secondary settings*. That is, they were more intense and imaginative than those around them The greatest part of your congregations like singing the hymns and are sometimes quite interested in your homilies. They are glad to do omnipresent administrative jobs around the parish—become senior and junior wardens, do a stint on the Worship and Growth committee, serve on a call committee, structure the annual meeting.

There is nothing about their apparent goals that speaks to recognition of a national moral crisis when it comes. For that matter, at the time when clergy now in their middle age were ordained, they would very likely not have had built into their training any expectation that they, themselves, would ever have to do anything to save the republic of the United States. It couldn't have been one of their career insights.

Clergy complain to one another, and unwisely, occasionally, to favorites among their lay people, about the loneliness of being clergy, especially in rural parishes. Passion about things Christian

---

[15] The piggery of Executive Incentive payment is impressive. Twenty years ago, most shareholders urging No votes at all were urging them on the line that promised the CEO 25 times as much as the average reimbursement of non-managerial wages in the firm. This year, 2005, some firms guarantee over 100 times the average non-managerial pay in order to give their Executives proper "incentive." Just to get it from the horse's mouth: A shareholder named The Catholic Funds, in Milwaukee, and the Sisters of St Joseph of Carondelet, St Louis Province, proposed to Citigroup: that the Board of Directors "limit the Compensation paid to the CEO in any fiscal year to no more than 100 times the average Compensation paid to the company's Non-Managerial Workers in the prior fiscal year, unless the shareholders have approved paying the CEO a greater amount..." to which Citygroup replied, "Citigroup's incentive compensation programs are designed to attract and retain talented executives..." and so forth. *March 15, 2005, announcement of Citigroup stockholders' meeting* to follow in April.

is a microscopic part of church life. However passionate the rector may be about, say, the marvelous insights and goals of New Testament writers, chances are that their parishioners only feel a somewhat bemused admiration of the rector for being so "on board" about Jesus.

A subtle and very modern application of the idea of *secondary settings*: assume that the neuroscientists of the 1990s and late 1980s are right: the neocortex constantly relays electrically fired "messages" between new perceptions and old stored values and old stored categories.[16] Let us assume neuroscience is right in saying our brains grab the aesthetic sensations from our perception centers and relay them back and forth in bands of consciousness across the 6-layered mantle of our classiest *thinking* brain part—in the end, at best, more often than we are disposed to believe, driving our mere aesthetic start-up to altruism. Altruism! If that is true, part of our potential *style* as homo sapiens is always to be entertaining strange combinations of thought up there under the rangy dome of the cranium. If we are always entertaining novel insights, then consciousness just in itself is a kind of secondary setting. As with all secondary settings, things are no longer so comfy as before, but much more interesting. [We refer enthusiastically to neuroscience because most people still discount the hard sciences as "reductive." They are not.]

If the ethically curious mind is a marvel to us, a new but friendly secondary setting, then certainly being a lot of the time in groups is really the reverse—a kind of ostracism of the soul. Young clergy complain of having no time for their own spirits. They probably ought to complain of that more rather than less, but presumably they don't dare. Maybe we all spend too much time in groups.

If we believe at all in psychological stage development we need to believe that at least some followers *may not want to stay*

---

[16] q.v. Gerald Edelman, MD, on "reentry," listed with other modern neuroscientists in the Appendix and William Wordsworth cited in the Appendix and Antonio Damasio, MD, in *The Feeling of What Happens* cited in the Appendix.

*stuck as followers*. Neuroscience suggests that being a leader, that is, a private person with a liking for the universe, is a predilection of the human cortex as it does its work above the merely practical nuclei of the brain. If this is true, followers by the hundreds of thousands and millions may all this time be longing, in their gray and white gel under the cranium, to become leaders.

## Part 2. Using Holy and Moral Language as Psychological Dynamics

> The kind of church-going that liberals scoff at has this virtue: for two hours a week, one hour of Sunday school and one hour of church, in the case of Protestant churches, words never heard in television dramas and sports reporting, and scarcely ever in most American homes, come crowding into children's ears....*Love, Service, Honor* and so forth become some kind of norm to any child hearing them repeated by adults outside the home (clergy and Sunday school teachers), provided they are adults whom the community seems to treat with respect.
>
> —Carol Bly, *Changing the Bully Who Rules the World*, Milkweed Press, 1996

It would be most helpful if liberal-arts-educated people would make more effort to be insightful instead of merely snobbish about bland language.

They allow themselves all sorts of dicta about mousy Midwestern speech (starting with Mari Sandoz, in *Old Jules*). They constantly remind us that British newspapers say things straight instead of pillowing everything in Latinate gas. It's all true, what they say, but it doesn't take into account the psychological or sociological pressures to use bland language.

TV, like death of any kind, is a great equalizer. In 2005 Oxford and UC Berkeley and Harvard and Stanford graduates use bland (also inchoate) language that any character from Huckleberry Hound to Twin Peaks to Seinfeld would feel at home with. One of the salient aspects of the infamous "dumbing down of America" is this all-population use of bland, or even worse, bland-plus-cute, language.

In the 1980s urban churches began advertising the week's sermon on marquee-like signs outside the building. Perhaps the clergy were anxious not to appear out-of-date to young parishioners lest they every week show up in still fewer numbers. The battle for flip phrasing was serious.

One cause of downgraded language is that beginning somewhere in the 1960s Americans took back their Sundays. It sounds all very freeing to leave off going to church. It is freeing, too. Now that everyone is in the workplace, it is pleasant to have Sunday mornings to oneself and one's family or friends. Quitting church deprived educated and educable Americans, however, of two powerful leadership tools: first, they lost hearing in their ears abstract words for virtue spoken loudly from lecterns. Children grew up having *never* heard abstract words for virtue and vice spoken loudly—or at all. Second, they lost the cultural model *for personal sacrifice.*

For a child, to imagine a man endangering himself in order to spare others is a very engaging idea. Nothing about what people talk about in church, especially Moses standing up to Pharoah or Jesus dying rather than capitulating, happens around town or suburb, or especially around farm yards where the death of familiar creatures is a mere practicality. It is practical that we raise animals specifically to be killed and then we eat them. This coupled with less and less teaching of American or any other history means fewer and fewer people actually imagining character.

An especially unattractive aspect of TV watching for children is the cynicism of most children's programs. Much invites scoffing and kidding. Little invites admiration. The neocortex, however, has some circuitry that brightens up around stories to admire, not to scoff at. I remember the first time I heard what rural families call "a family story." A family story is usually an anecdote to kid about. It is usually an anecdote about someone of a recent past generation whom we were to regard as "a character." Story: A great uncle of someone, while the other hands and the farmer himself were resting at midday in the field because you had to rest the team animals, threw a cup of hot coffee into the face of one of the mules. It cried out. In the next minute it died. The man telling the story laughed and gave his head a shake. "Nope," he said, "he was quite a character." In my mind I saw the mule. To this day I see that mule. But we were asked to smile at the great-uncle because he was quite a character.

One needs high-minded narrative, not cynical stories, to make people leaders. So it is too bad about the church going. No matter how stupid the pastor or priest or rabbi, he or she would never ask you to grin at a story about cruelty. Clergy are there to show the flag for kindness and they generally do it.

Granted, church can be blindingly stupid. For that reason or to save time, each year fewer people go to services. Great words for mercy and justice are in that way disappearing from normal life. Great models of self-sacrifice are disappearing.

What is left is a phenomenon that throughout history is associated with empires: life spent mostly in the presence of others. Slaves and poor people are usually dumped into groups, but now, as our species over-populates the world, students and even the well-to-do must spend ever more time in one another's presence. Life, being so heavily social, means life largely spent with very little contrast and individuality because group life works only *if there isn't much contrast inside the group.*[17]

Goals larger than one's own life grow faint, because larger-than-life goals are by definition passionate—such as mathematical truth and religious ideas—and passionate ideas are divisive and groups do poorly with diverse members. This is unconsciously understood by young people. Instead of making themselves be empathic with the "different" people, however, they solve the problem by themselves being vague—vague enough so they are neither *like* others nor *different* from them. Their lack of definition is sometimes quite surrealistic. For example, young people in 1970 began saying "I'm like, what's going on?" Or "I'm like, don't go there." What is peculiar about those two phrases is

---

[17] This is the covert reason soldiers wear uniforms.

that they absolutely avoid naming any *emotion*. One cannot jeer at or ostracize someone who has just said, "When you say stuff like that, I am like what's going on?" That is language used as a seat belt.

There is something else one cannot do with people who have just said that: one can't really even guess what they actually *are* thinking or feeling. If one can't guess, one can't know them. If they themselves can't guess what they are feeling, they, too, don't know themselves very well. If no one is quite sure what they themselves or the others are thinking and feeling, then we live in a psychological lagoon where no crystals form and no currents move and nothing under the lukewarm surface is identified. It is like swimming in a warm pond and feeling something a little alien, someone's leg perhaps, sliding against ours, but not necessarily a human leg. Perhaps it has fur. Perhaps it has scales. You can't know what the creature's size is—you can't know how much of its body touched you. Maybe it was enormous. Maybe what grazed you was only tail or fin. Another thing: you aren't quite sure it was alive. It might have been a giant, which in its dying, slid silkily against your body.

If too much of our talking life is guesswork, repetitive, but still guesswork, one hesitates a good deal before doing anything that isn't exactly what one's neighbors are doing. When intense language is not in our brains we must do without it. The brain will have to take guidance from dumber parts of itself.

Low below the fiery six layers of cortex lie the unconscious but dutiful engine-running nuclei, amygdalae and cingulate, for example, the parts that always vote for homeostasis—the same temperature, no changes, please; the same humidity, the same quantity and general type of nutrient sources, the expected ranges of noise and brightness entering at the perception centers. Like the valves and dials of a ship's engine room, these parts of the brain do honorable work maintaining the organism as well as they can. They've never met the captain. They don't need to. They do not work at *consciousness*. Their choices are all to do with maintenance.

When human society loses fervor, it slips downwards and backwards into mere maintenance. Engineering instead of mathematics. Gourmet cooking instead of philosophy. Perhaps people do maintenance with flare but maintenance is still maintenance.

Mere maintenance is a new low, as cultural ideals go. Maintenance, however, is right in our faces. The swift moves, the symbolism of words—let's face this—don't brighten millions of our minds.

Possibly, church clergy people could do a lot to reverse this loss of *the abstract language of virtue*. I don't think churches can reverse the horrible loss of solitude. Social workers are telling us very clearly that so little solitude remains for our adolescents that it is hard for them to progress *through* adolescence, as civilized people must, in order to be emotionally and intellectually in touch *with their own minds*. Social workers say that and write it, but larger forces than they are dumping American young people into ever larger and larger groups right along.[18]

One can't win all the battles at once. For now, the best clergy can do about language is to use the language of their own passionate profession, and reject the business and not-for-profit organizational language that has crept into their speech in the last decades.

Here is a little list of business and junk-organizational language.

| JUNK PHRASING | HOW IT IS USED |
| --- | --- |
| Concern. Concerned | —a euphemism for terrified, anxious, fearful, infuriated |
| Comfortable with | —a euphemism for morally willing, ethically indifferent |
| Challenged | —not as intelligent as would be useful in the particular situation |

---

[18] q.v. Kathy Emery and Susan Ohanian, *Why is Corporate America Bashing Our Public Schools?* Portsmouth, NH: Heinemann, A Division of Reed Elsevier Inc., 361 Hanover St., Portsmouth, NH 03801-3912, © 2004.

Struggling —failing, losing

Productive —clear, effective, decent, kind

Inappropriate —This is the all-purpose word in the lexicon of people who dare to criticize a behavior, but mean to sound objective about it

Most of this language was invented in corporate or non-profit organizations, but some comes from pro-football. Teams are said to "struggle" if their quarterback is considered "challenged." People who do not read literature tend to trust TV announcers. They model their own language on them. So it would be very hard to convince most congregations to use passionate language for any particular reason. Bland language is all that followers have. It is also used by leaders: our business-oriented culture battens on it. When people use bland language the language itself mutes strong symbols in their minds. When clergy write to the Senate in bland language, Senators will not think they're crazy. But no one with power like Senators' power reads much of the mail and the people who sort through their mail for them glaze while breasting through the warm pond of bland words.

Let us say you actually feel equable about William Pryor's urging Congress to eliminate the provision of the Voting Rights Act that protects the right to vote for racial minorities. Pryor labeled that provision "an affront to federalism and an expensive burden that has far outlived its usefulness." In Hope v. Pelzer Pryor defended Alabama's practice of handcuffing prison inmates to outdoor hitching posts without access to water if they refused to work on chain gangs. He also represented the only state of the United States to challenge the constitutionality of the federal remedy for victims of sexual assault and violence in the Violence Against Women Act (U.S. v. Morrison).[19] If you feel unaffected

---

[19] Fact sheet of Leadership Conference on Civil Rights (LCCR/LCCREF). The website also gives an extensive list of organizations opposing the lifetime appointment of Pryor. He was a recess appointment by George W. Bush on 2-20-04.

by these particular stands of William Pryor's there is no point to writing a Senator about him. But if you are outraged or saddened or horrified, then these are the words to use when you address yourself to a Senator:

> Outrage
> Sadness
> Horror
> Grief

Americans don't use strong enough language when angry, nor strong enough language when they praise. [Further, far too few letters or telephone calls of praise get made to Senators. Perhaps it is not a shocker that Senator Robert C. Byrd gets so much mail as he gets, but that he doesn't get more. It is a shocker the praise such a Senator *doesn't* get.]

Let's say that you, an educated clergy person, were delighted that Supreme Court Justice Anthony M. Kennedy wrote the majority opinion (5-4) in abolishing capital punishment for juvenile offenders. He wrote: "From a moral standpoint, it would be misguided to equate the failings of a minor with those of an adult, for a greater possibility exists that a minor's character deficiencies will be reformed." He further said that "Our determination finds confirmation in the stark reality that the United States is the only country in the world that continues to give official sanction to the juvenile death penalty."[20] If you were delighted, Justice Kennedy wants thanking. When the United States takes some decent measure about something, and you consequently feel gratified and respectful, then when writing whichever legislator or judge or agent of the United States who did this act, words of praise should be intense words like:

> Esteem
> Joy
> Gratitude finally

---

[20] Supreme Court decision March 1, 2005, Roper v Simmons. The others in the majority were John Paul Stevens, David H. Souter, Ruth Bader Ginsburg, and Stephen G. Breyer.

Use of strong words further increases one's own taste for strong feelings. You might have a look at one or more books of the neuroscientist Gerald M Edelman.[21] He describes electro-chemical connection-making between the perception centers of the brain and the neuronal groups who keep bands of consciousness flying between what you are seeing at this moment and what you have seen before and what moves you mortally now that moved you less strongly or more strongly before, or exactly the same before. This is a process Dr. Edelman calls *re-entry*. We think Edelman writes most beautifully about it in two of his books: *Bright Air, Brilliant Fire* and *A Universe of Consciousness*. Strong language, which means, almost invariably, language closer to the actual feeling or concept felt, reassures the brain that you who use words like "mercy", "justice", and "cruelty" have a stake in such stuff.

If that sounds odd, turn this observation backside to: Weak language, such as "don't go there" without anyone's defining what the *there* is that we are *uncomfortable* with, tells the brain that 98.6 is what we do, don't go there if it's not 98.6. O don't go there, Soul. In fact, Soul, most of your urges are uncomfortable! Don't go along with them!

What we are asking you to do, then, is to write and speak to your Senators and members of the Senate Judiciary Committee in the language natural to people who, in truth, seriously hate cruelty.

---

[21] See bibliography for mention of Dr Edelman's work.

# Part 3. Courage as the third psychological property of leadership

You clergymen or clergywomen don't need much courage in your daily ministry.

The author of Psalm 23 may have had his table "spread in the presence of his enemies" but yours isn't. If the congregation aren't all profound friends at least they are the people who hired you. What they hired you for is work among friends, not squaring up to enemies and crying out for justice. They want you to assuage their abraded feelings about their own lives. They want you to help them develop right feeling about life's occasions. That's a friendly enough task and deeply, profoundly worth doing.

It is especially hard to soothe Americans' feelings right now. We are crowded and losing pride and our schools are too crowded to make much dent in ignorance. People are not stupid. They feel abraded by all this. The Buddhists' "Eightfold Path" includes Right Thinking, as do all religions, but your parishioners know it is hard to do when more and more people have to accommodate the criminal practices of businesses. People are not free to resign from cruel organizations unless they have private means. Even executives are not free to interrupt a meeting with, "Are we sure we want to do this?" And finally, many of us slip into cutting a few ethical corners in order to make it *at all* in our system.

I remember once learning that a farmer in Lac Qui Parle County, MN, tried to sell sick animals and got caught by a state inspector. He sat in church, too artless to sell his sick animals without getting caught, next to people who got away with what they did. That's parish life, as you know.

Please especially notice: those sitting in your congregations consist of victims of bad corporate or government-agency behavior and also those who themselves do the organizing and clipping and bullying. There they are, all of them glad to be listening to you. They may be partly bored, but not completely bored. Such parishioners of yours as do the dirty work of the USA workplace all week, Monday through Friday, may do a lot of fair or merciful work as well,[22] but they acquiesce in their workplace wrongdoing, too. They want your sermons.

They wait gladly as you give out the week's harmless announcements. They are glad of your forthright voice as you read aloud from either Testament. They count on you to *neutralize* their caustic life, Monday through Friday. Ralph Waldo Emerson gave a speech to the senior class of the Harvard Divinity School in 1838 in which he told these soon-to-be clergy not to "be too anxious to visit periodically all families and each family in your parish connection" but rather "when you meet one of these men or women...let their timid aspirations find in you a friend; let their trampled instincts be genially tempted out in your atmosphere."[23] They tend, like any American, not to have any sense of what's going on in their unconscious minds, but they have inklings and rumblings from inside there. Emerson believed that if a man is dishonest—let's you and I put it broadly and say *crooked*—he loses consciousness of himself. "If a man dissemble, deceive, he deceives himself *and goes out of acquaintance with his own being* [our emphasis]." This intuitive psychological insight was made a century and a half before neuroscience began to discern, by their envisioning machinery, how inside our neocortices the fiery contagion of thought is actually lessened or increased by our behaviors, defenses—by our mentoring, or the lack of mentoring—or by wrong mentoring.

Your parishioners count on you to neutralize the acid of their lives.

They hired you for that. They pay you either tens of thousands or hundreds of thousands of dollars to do that for them. They know you won't discount their griefs.

---

[22] For a surrealistic experience, go to the website of several corporations whose top people have in the last 5 years been caught stealing from pension funds and in other thievery. It is an eye opener to see how younger executives participate in all sorts of community projects. It is an eye opener to see listed the handouts those companies make over to local communities.

[23] Ralph Waldo Emerson, "An Address," Harvard Divinity School, Sunday evening, July 15, 1838.

In return for your kindness they generally do you the kindness of not criticizing you for being dull or chicken-hearted or any of the other objections that people have to clergy. People who make a lot of money tend to believe that people who make comparatively little money take up an idealistic profession just because they haven't the skill or moxie to work the system. They will hide any superior feelings like that, if they have them. A good many of them may very well not want anything one could call spiritual insight anyway. They rather like it when you say simple things and when you reiterate doctrines that mankind has doubted the truth of for hundreds of years.

In addition to neutralizing the bitter smog of American culture in their minds they of course expect you to bury their dead and to perform marriage ceremonies so cheerful that for that half-hour or hour people can keep their minds free of the undertows of thought.

People who are not ordained clergy only *appear* to respect clergy more than they respect non-clergy. I think we make a mistake to think there is much admiration there. Laypeople cling around clergy because they are wistful for that confident belief that life is nicer than it is, a tone given off by you when you move kindly through the after-service coffee hour in your cassock. Actually they may smile at you a lot because you symbolize goodness. Most of them probably like you personally. Even the few of them who want you out of there aren't a serious threat. None of them wants to destroy you financially so they can eat up your assets and take the place where you stand.

There's no danger in your life.

You scarcely have to worry about losing your job, an increasing likelihood for other adult Americans.

Administration is followers' work but you have to do a lot of it. You take aboard the values of the church and the more exemplary values of the local community and manage your organization as well as you can. It is wonderful work. Much work of non-leaders *is* wonderful. The point is that most of it is of less vital importance than leaders' work.

Let me explain by hypothesizing the whole United States as a community. The United States, like any city, like the countryside with its methane-filled prisons for hogs, has some appalling values. Some United States values are secretly evil but brightly spray-painted to look good. Some are genuinely exemplary values. We can each make our own list of what's appalling, what's phony, and what's really ethical. One favorite value of do-gooders in the United States is the idea that *all* their various projects are valuable and wonderful. Saving the environment, saving vanishing species, preventing over-fishing of hake and salmon, being careful to discard electric batteries separately from ordinary trash—these are good and valuable but each of them is much less valuable than other good work. In fact, if hypothetical evildoers could be certain that the only opposition they would get was people demonstrating on overpass bridges or saving moribund species and the like, they could do nearly anything they liked. No one would be eagerly addressing the Congress in an effort to remove power from them or keep them from being appointed to power.

Followers hate this kind of prioritizing of civic ethical actions because openly opposing the enemy by name is scarier and harder work and less sure of immediate success than picking up trash on the beach. Hence the unwillingness throughout modern life in republics (where people have any say at all) to making critical distinctions between genial, small activities and outright opposition to national leaders. I brought this up because the clergy so uniformly follow the general virtue-code of making no distinctions between useful leadership activities and well-meant followership activities.

What we are asking you to do, saving the Judiciary system, however, is leaders' work and it must be done alone or at least with not more than 2 or 3 of you joining in your approach to the Senators.

It seems to us that you will need these kinds of courage:

1.  Resistence to scorn—

    You may be scorned by your own parishioners if they find out you are doing it. If hundreds of American clergy start pressing on Senators to care for the Judiciary it will be noticeable and your church council or senior wardens may ask you if you are one of those. If you say yes they may consider that treachery. They regard you as their hireling, hired to neutralize the bitter feelings in their daily lives. This actively going to Senators is not neutralizing anything.

2.  Saying what you mean—

    If you use strong and feeling language, such language as blooms in words like mercy, cruelty, justice, and injustice, you may at first offend the Senators you are in touch with, but later, perhaps, not. It is important to remember that at any one time many Senators are ashamed of what their Party makes them do, and your language may wake up more deeply-sourced feelings in them.

3.  Giving yourself to a losing cause—

    You may lose. Americans have always disliked losers. I don't know any American history given to young people that tells them that Jefferson spent the last 17 years of his life in deep sorrow and unease.[24] He was so aware of how the continent enticed people to the West, and of the people no longer caring about the Constitution, especially about the rights of man which meant so much to him. You may actually be asked to leave your church for reasons which will be variously worded. The gist of it will be that you took it upon yourself to stand apart from the crowd. You acted on national rather than parish principles. Your congregation did not identify your doing that as being about your Father's

---

[24] See page 12 for additional information on this.

business, so to speak. Ordinary non-readers generally don't like any kind of intellectuals very well anyway. Intellectuals talk about *invisible* things. Well, they like intellectuals even less when they are *moral* intellectuals. Recall how enraged Harvard was at Emerson's 1838 "Address at Divinity College" in which he inveighed against lifelessness in the church. It took Harvard 28 years to get over their huff and give Emerson the honor so long due him. For every reinstatement to respect like Emerson's at Harvard there are likely thousands of cases of fine people who stood against mediocrity or stood up on behalf of some just cause, lost, and sank into disappointment. That may happen to you. There are few jobs about, and if you leave your church, you run the chance of not getting another one. And what are you trained for except the church? You wouldn't be any good at selling products you don't believe in. You wouldn't be any good at torturing prisoners. You wouldn't be any good at lying adroitly so that your company's entire pension fund melts into lava.

4. Taking your chances with the powers that be—

You may attract unpleasant notice from the Homeland Security. If you had gone around with a sign in the National Mall and ridden in the bus that someone is going to collect $100,000 for, you wouldn't have been of any interest to them. Bus riders are followers, at least so long as they herd around on buses. See the discussion and note on page 22.

5. Facing the likelihood that bullies never respond to molly-handling—

How different your speaking directly to Senators will be from signing pleas designed to waken conscience in the President! This difference is a profound division between leaders and followers. Leaders make themselves face the horrifying truth that there is no point in writing letters to this President. He wants to be doing what he is doing. He and some of his coterie nearly glisten now that they are so powerful. If power is what someone wants, what more could he or she ask for than at home to dismantle the freedoms of the greatest republic in the world, and abroad to attack any country he or she chooses to attack. People bent to fulfill dreams like that would only grin at letters that aim to prick their consciences—especially letters written as mere pleas without muscle.

A hypothetical example will make it clear. Facts: in 1942 Field Marshall Paulus begged Hitler several times to let him retreat with his men because they were losing at Stalingrad. The army was both freezing and starving. At one point a German relief force was actually within hailing distance—but Hitler would not even allow Paulus to lead his dying 6th army over to the others who had food, medicine, shelter, and means to get home. Hitler had decided he wanted Paulus and his men to stand and die, all of them, at Stalingrad.

Now let us fantasize that someone, or perhaps a group of mothers of men on the Eastern Front, wrote the letter below. And suppose they felt it would add strength to their plea if hundreds of others signed. So they went about on foot, on what bikes still had tires, on still-running streetcars, and got signatures.

Mein Führer!

Wir wenden uns an Sie mit der Bitte,
Feldmarschall Paulus und der Sechsten Armee
den Rückzug von Stalingrad zu erlauben,
um weiteres Sterben unter Erfrieren der dort
stationierten Soldaten zu verhindern. Bitte
verwenden Sie die Züge mit denen derzeit Juden
nach Auschwitz transportiert werden, um unsere
Soldaten nach Hause zu bringen, solange dies
noch möglich ist.

[My Fuehrer! We are coming to you with the plea that you allow Field Marshal Paulus and the 6th Army to retreat from Stalingrad, in order to prevent further death and freezing among the soldiers stationed there. Please convert the trains now being used to transport Jews to Auschwitz to the task of bringing our soldiers home, so long as this is still possible.]

Because such a letter would have been written over a half-century ago and in a country far away, it gives us perspective enough to recognize how little attention a determined power lover pays to beggars! How scornful Hitler might feel, if such a letter somehow got through to him at all.

It is followers' mindset to go into serious denial about the pleasure that a bully gets from causing deaths by the tens of thousands! Followers would be depressed to read the more jubilant letters of Napoleon. When followers spend time signing their names to pleas to great bullies they are pretending to themselves that the world is so kind that major bullies can be turned around by pleas. Actually, pleading most typically whets a bully's lust to bash the victims in question some more. Ivan the Terrible used to make priests watch his palace soldiers torture people because it buttressed his excitement in two ways: first, he got to do the torture, which he regularly enjoyed, and second, he got to watch the priests wriggle in fear for themselves and in shame that they couldn't make themselves shout against their Czar.

Followers wouldn't touch the work we hope you will do.

You and we know that holy language is very out of style now. Still, here is a too-little noticed glimmer of life: people over 45 or 50, in their millions, long for sounds of holiness. They long for them because they remember them. In fact, holiness as a back-up plan, so to speak, lingers in middle-aged people's heads. They still know, half-consciously at least, that it is unholy and wicked for a republic to take away the freedoms of others. They don't find it "inappropriate" or "a matter of concern" to take away these freedoms. They find it evil.

If you, then, use the deepest language of your profession instead of groupy schmooze you may have some chance with our United States Senators.

## An Empathy-Based Stage-Development Theory
### —An Introduction

Oddly enough, human beings' brains are specified for the potential to want mercy for people and creatures they have never met and never will. It seems like an extraordinarily pleasant thing to say about our species. It certainly seems like a potential to be glad of.

There is, as always with any mere potential for one or another virtue or vice, a proviso: human beings do not fulfill their potential for imagination—empathy being a use of imagination—*unless they are taught in words.* That is, the brain is dynamic. It alters its capabilities as it chooses which hundreds of its connections to focus on, to be conscious of. It discounts thousands every several milliseconds. On a hot afternoon, a group of neurons suggest to their host, a bored young person, that he or she step on a passing ant. That particular young person, however, recalling Aesop on ants and grasshoppers, sees the hard-labor aspect of the ant as it tears along on its tactile feet. The young person spends a moment thinking about ants generally, not with any particular respect. This child's not a fool. He or she knows that an ant's options appear to be very second-rate in comparison to a human being's options; human beings in a democracy or a republic can't be sent 24/7 on errands. Consciousness of an ant en passant, imagining whatever part of its life we can't estimate on the spot—all we see is the ant dashing along— is more interesting than a jolt to the amygdala or cingulate from stepping on it. Here is what has just happened: core consciousness has swerved along some mentored pathways (pathways nourished by stories heard) and in doing so has discounted or devalued the old casual idea of killing a small passing other because you can. Any individual neuron, it is interesting to note, fires up many times faster than consciousness itself fires up. Milliseconds is what a neuron needs: consciousness takes whole seconds. Of course, because consciousness is based on thousands of neurons, in groupings, racing in bands across the cerebral cortex, making connections, not only between early sensory cortices and remembered perceptions from another time, but between this moment's early sensory cortices and remembered past perceptions and remembered invisible values put on those past perceptions. This is the potential we are given.

Anyone can see, however, that the pathway takes privilege—the privilege of having been mentored, having been told stories, not having been scorned so often that scorn itself is what we've learnt. When an organism (that's we ourselves) has been more scorned than mentored, the imagination to query what an ant may be doing as we pass it is not developed enough to overcome the Jungle programming. We are, as the helping professionals would put it, at risk to step on the ant.

Years ago, *The New York Times* published on page A-1 a picture of first-graders in a public school. They had their lower arms dutifully upon their desktops, hands clasped, for the class photograph. The picture showed an extraordinarily beautiful child in the foreground. Not only were her forehead and eyebrows and eyes and delicate mouth perfect, but her expression was full of anticipation. School was terrific for her. The picture showed her marvelous joy in learning. It was the kind of face first-grade teachers rejoice in. The picture accompanied an essay on the subject of Manhattan's vast shortage of school social workers. A worker had reported suspicious particulars about that little girl, but there had been no appropriate follow-up. This particular child had been beaten so frequently by her mother that she died not long after the school picture was taken. Hers was a chilling case of an entire organism—a whole human being— with its classical, cerebral potential of our species, destroyed by environment.

It's important to keep two neurological insights in mind at the same time: the good news, the brain, in a sense parallel to the entire person, is programmed with the potential of altruism and love of complex thinking and fine-tuned feelings. The bad news: the brain, as does an entire person, gets served a huge range of very bad luck to medium bad luck to good luck to extraordinarily good luck. A child gradually killed by her mother had been dealt very bad luck. Well then: if the brain has the potential for imagining creatures and people far away and wishing them fairness and mercy as they go about their lives, a good many millions of brains have been dealt some sorts of bad luck. That is, a good many millions, or even billions, of brains have not fulfilled any such imaginative and altruistical potential. The organisms (people) to whom those brains belong have been halted. In the New York case of cruelty, the entire child died. In millions of other cases, only a child's brain is endangered or ruined by cruelty in the environment.

What is jungle? Jungle philosophy is practical and it is inherited. No one inherits an imaginative philosophy. It is only a potential.

When there is a failure of potential, it is tremendously helpful to follow a model of analysis that classical theology and classical social work oddly share: namely, instead of our exclaiming, "For goodness' sake how did this person turn out so awful?" the better question is "How has this person, at least so far as he or she has gotten in life, gotten so stalled from more admirable stages of development?"

Much of neurology has been learnt by neurosurgeons looking into not normal brains but damaged brains. Much of moral psychology has been learnt by looking into cases of moral failure. We start, then, by how and perhaps why human endeavor has *failed* in a particular instance. Therefore, let us assume that imagination is a potential for everyone: then why hasn't this person shown any signs of imagination?

If it seems obstinate to work in a frame of failure, it sometimes helps to look back on your own childhood or what you know of someone else's childhood. For example, all ethical or moral quality comes to our consciousness for the first time when we recognize its *absence*, not its presence. [Nearly all pleasant presences in a child's life, such as kind parents and a clean place to sleep, are so normalized to the child that he or she takes no notice of them.] How different it is with unpleasant occasions! When a child for the first time is blamed for some behavior that another child did, our child shouts, "That's not fair!" "Not Fair!" Until then whatever the mother or father or caretaker did had no particular moral quality. It was simply part of the general universe of parents or caretakers. The way things are...the way parents are. Static, and not attracting one's notice. Now that the child has been outraged, however, that child knows that even if much of life remains ethically neutral, simply the way things are, some is *not*: at a given moment parents and caretakers are either just or unjust. A child feeling this has just made a leap forward in his or her potential for ethics. Some things are still just nature—but now some other things are good or bad.

But we feel diffident at drawing a likeness between even one theological concept and any social work method of client treatment. We know perfectly well how cross most educated people are with most church doctrine. Please know that we know that, and be tolerant of, if not one whit grateful for, a smart theological idea from long ago.

Here it is. Sin is classically regarded as shortfall from virtue, rather than as merely an evil propensity or behavior. So far as Christian theology goes, the devil is not equal and opposite to God, but a fallen angel whose doings are a matter of shortfall from what angels' behaviors ought to be. The idea is medieval, but intuitive thinkers showed up a thousand years ago and ten times as long before that. The idea of jungle behavior being a shortfall from neocortex idealism is quite wonderful. For readers who know John Milton's *Paradise Lost* the idea of shortfall in an angel won't be new. The average Christian of our time is cheerfully ignorant of any past psychological insights in Christian theology. Too bad. This one about shortfall is therapeutic. If you take it aboard it is like a compass in hand before getting into a lifeboat mid-ocean. What you are up against is still extraordinarily dangerous and close to death but you can plan a route. This is the lesson social workers buck up their youngest clients with.

Classically, a worker regards a child as deprived of or otherwise blocked from, for an example, the sentience a human being needs in order to be reasonably, sociably thoughtful of others. The worker goes about probing here and there to see exactly which property of psychological development that child needs in the way of back and fill.

We commend shortfall from the ideal as a cognitively useful way to see what empathic stage-development philosophy is about.

Shortfall from the ideal has been the method of medical research. Much of neurology has been learnt by neurosurgeons' seeing which damage, where, caused a given patient's failure, or shortfall. We are asking ourselves to do a process like that—to start with a lack, in the case of this book and this particular stage-development scheme, that lack being imagination and the altruism so often consequent to imagination. It seems obstinate deliberately to work in a frame of failure, but we remind ourselves that all ethical quality first comes to our consciousness when it has failed us.

In our stage-development scheme, we will describe six stages and discuss some circumstances that keep people stuck in the practical jungle of stages 1 and 2 and other circumstances that release people to somehow get through stages 3 and 4. In these stages, 3 and 4, when the soul longs to feel "supported" in the arms of peers, and fervent in taking guidance from leaders, the personality still is making its decisions in a growling, convulsed style.

Only in stage 5 does a person imagine oneself imagining the world instead of imagining oneself only behaving and feeling this way or that way. Once the imagination has lurched past one's closer-in influences—the classmates, the local leaders, the national leaders as they choose to portray themselves—only then do people weigh distant, eternal, conceptual truths into their decision-making. Socrates wouldn't have cared two tetradrachms' worth for the "examined life" if he hadn't meant examining a wide range of it, not just whatever stood about the local parish.

But there is no money in stage 5 scope of attention and then feeling and then thinking, as the conversationalists in *The Republic* and *Meno* liberally pointed out to Socrates. The Athens of Socrates was no longer the deeply admired, ingeniously-invented democracy of the Greeks. In a government with heavy leanings toward empire, no politician in his or her right mind would give 20 seconds' airspace to an appeal for stage 5 thinking. No power-addicted government has any admiration for empathically imagining invisible others. As for voting kindly fates for invisible people (or the earth far away from our back yards), to a power enthusiast such an idea is like telling grandpa on his eightieth that he looks as good as ever.

Still, this is 21st-century America that we are living in, not 22nd-century America. In our time there are still hundreds of thousands of stage 5 people around. These people are fools if they tell themselves that our republic looks as good as ever, but if they are not fools they look around and without denial they see, near at hand, people appearing to have gotten stuck in the jungle mentality. Like other mammals we biologically inherit parts of the brain other than the neocortex. If you pay no attention to what the neocortex has to offer (and if you don't allow it any education) you are reduced to the wisdom of much less evolved parts of the brain. Those parts are straight jungle.[25]

## A quick definition of Straight Jungle

- You want it, you grab it.
- If someone prevents you from grabbing it, hurt them until they let go.
- If you feel bored and are big enough to carry it off, bite someone outside the tribe.

---

[25] A curious note that applies to "straight jungle." Professor John Dolan of the University of Minnesota Department of Philosophy pointed out how often, when a totally selfish, pre-philosophical, pre-moral sort of behavior was criticized by university philosophers, non-philosophers would jeer, crying "Look—join the Real World why don't you!" I found it very interesting that jungle (self-serving) behavior protects itself by claiming *reality*.

- If you are not big enough to extort from others, try to get big enough so you can.
- In things to do with affection: get big enough so you have power enough to channel to *your* loved ones, away from someone *else's* loved ones, such blessings as that someone else still has hold of.

## Stages 1 and 2 versus Hans Christian Andersen

Stages 1 and 2 are the practical stages. Stage 1 people are 100% practical for the reasons a baby of any species is practical. It breastfeeds when hungry. People in stage 2, the tribal-loyalty stage, serve their loved ones with more "unconditional love" than in other stages. The whole idea of "unconditional love" is a tribal stage 2 idea. What it says is let's not do any criticism close in. Anybody in our space is safe from standards of behavior.

A greater fault of stage 2 people is that they serve *only* their loved ones. All more distant relationships tend to be like nations' foreign policies. They are informed by psychological nervousness in which a couple of the brain's limbic centers ask, a) is there a threat to me and mine out there? And b) is there any way I can cadge some of what those neighbors have and haul it back home for me and mine?

Most Grimm Brothers folktales are stage 2 stories. It's important to notice that though the recognizable offenders are German peasants, royalty in those tales are in stage 2 as well. That's the nature of folk tales, as opposed to more profound literature. There's one good brother. The other brother tries to steal from him. All strangers are suspect. Trickery on behalf of oneself and one's family is good. Kings and Queens do trickery, too.

The Tribal stage two-edness of most orally told stories is awesome. It is rather horrible, just as most, not all, but most, family stories meant to regale people at reunions are horrible—that is, people are regarded as "quite a character." It is usually made clear that no one may talk philosophically about that person. No one is invited to think about what psychological dynamics were played out through that person. If you compare a Hans Christian Andersen fairy tale with a genuine German or Scandinavian folktale, you can see that Andersen is about mercy and justice for those who cannot get it for themselves because so much of the world, especially those with power, are Straight Jungle. That, by the way, is an essential difference between serious art and folk or street wisdom or family traditions. Art reminds us of our moral longings.

Art at its best rises above robust mockery. If this sounds strange, think of Chaucer's tales. How much pleasure do women take from reading Chaucer? In his lifetime, 1340? to 1400, Europe and England produced serious stage 5 people who longed for fairness. But Chaucer had the minstrel mentality: you make amusement for established privileged people to enjoy. There will always be room for that, for the same reason every small town has a happy-hour bar. People want a break from truth tellers like Andersen. Especially in a fun-loving near-empire, someone like the author of "The Ugly Duckling" can be a real drag.

## Secondary Versus Primary Consciousness

Unfortunately, despite our potential for examining life it is "the unexamined life," as Socrates called it, that most human beings live out. We unconsciously feel, however, that a mix of perceptions, garnered from our "early" sensory cortices, then flung together with previous perceptions, then all that relaying and reentering of the brain's various takes on the subject—that mix of activity all happening in milliseconds—should be ours. Lions don't do secondary consciousness. Dogs don't. But we do, and there is a variety of evidence showing that human beings feel resentment when they get no mentoring in things of our imaginations, or don't get taught to do such all-across-the-head thinking.[26]

In our stage-development scheme, as mentioned above, we will discuss a few of the circumstances that keep people from fulfilling the six stages that we see as available potential to human beings.

The general idea of the 1990s and 2000s in neurology is that only people, not animals, so far as we can tell, have secondary consciousness: that is, only people are conscious not just of what they see and hear and remember previously seeing and hearing—dogs do that much—but people are conscious of themselves as selves seeing and hearing and recalling and judging and deciding what kinds of lives to live. That suggests one reason, at least, why people behave so badly when deprived of imaginative life.

Animals and plants appear to be naturally practical. They appear to make impressive, even scary, adaptations to their environments so that they can survive the better. Perfect examples are the Utricula (bladderwort) and the Aldrovanda (the waterwheel). Both fool and capture small prey such as mosquito larvae, zooplankton and fish fry. That kind of thing. People, too, if you don't read their books and don't happen to hear them participating in mathematics or philosophy, probably look only practical to anyone observing us from outside. "O Look," the observers might be saying, as they go skimming by our Milky Way, "Wow, there's your jungle adaptation all right!"

---

[20] Please see in G. Edelman's *Bright Air, Brilliant Fire* a wonderful discussion of primary versus secondary consciousness. In Antonio Damasio's *The Feeling of What Happens* there is a careful, and—for which we are grateful—*accessible* description of the vital difference between mere alertness and consciousness. Please see the bibliography. For evidence of deprivation of imaginative development, please note discussions in *Pediatrics, Vol. 113 No. 4 April, 2004*, pages 708-713. The article proposes a possible danger of a child's brain, over-stimulated by television, getting permanently "rewired" when it ought, instead, to be developing. The American Academy of Pediatrics said in 1999 that children under the age of two should not watch TV at all because of possible deleterious effect upon early brain growth and the development of social, emotional, and cognitive skills. Their discussion was conducted by Dimitri A. Christakis, M.D., MPH, Dept. of Pediatrics, University of Washington; Frederick J. Zimmerman, PhD, Child Health Institute, David L. DiGiuseppe, Msc, Dept. of Health Services, the foregoing all at the University of Washington,; and Carolyn A. McCarty, PhD, Children's Hospital and Regional Medical Center, Seattle, WA. Heartbreaking observations have been arrived at and documented by The Kaiser Family Foundation and Children's Digital Media Centers, which found that kids in the 6-months to 6-year age group spend about two hours a day watching TV. One-third of children 6 years old and younger have TVs in their rooms. A similar proportion live in homes where a TV is on most or all of the time. In homes in which the TV is on all the time, only 34% of children in ages 4-6 can read, compared with 56% in homes where the TV is on less of the time.

## Our Present Culture Fails Most American Children

Our present culture fails most of its children. It doesn't educate them for their full imaginative potential. We know that, even without reading those educators who constantly warn us, but it is hard to say it aloud to oneself. American family life, shredded by television watching, is failing American children. American public schools, disfunded down to too few teachers to teach groups small enough to teach at all, fails American children.[27]

## Boredom as a Sign and Result of Blocked Imagination

Our brains have the specific potential for contemplation and evaluation of new perceptions. Those who say that one person is naturally imaginative and another is not are mistaken. This using our heads for contemplation and evaluation along with constantly revising or killing off old opinions or igniting new ones, all this kind of philosophical thing, is being described ever more intricately by neurologists. Some describe imaginative activity with special focus on the chemistry involved. Some describe imaginative activity in terms of structured pathways of neurons. Our heritage is to have been dealt out imaginative potential. If we don't use that imagination—call it evaluative connection making—our brains get intensely bored.

Mammals cotton to the slob pleasure of lying about in the heat of the day, but to actually feel bored is not pleasant to beast or homo sapiens. It's a bad feeling. The dullest creatures reach for any break to the boredom. They take drugs of choice. They overeat. Others indulge in violent fantasy, such as watching American television violence. Even a two-or three-year-old is at some risk to making a smaller or same-sized child give out a sharp cry of pain.

---

[27] The best recent book about this, that we have seen, because it is chock full of facts about our public schools and chock full of appropriate fury by its teacher-authors: Kathy Emery and Susan Ohanian, *Why is Corporate America Bashing our Public Schools?*

A purpose of culture is to heighten the imagination for the sake of a less boring life. Educated people read and tell classical stories to children. All Americans, because of democratic legislation in the 19$^{th}$ century, must go to school, where, if the school is one of the remaining good ones, children learn to make fast ties between perceptions (sight, sound, taste, etc.) and universal concepts. Concepts are more interesting than gouging, so most lucky children become socialized enough to enjoy imaginative work more than sadism, at least most of the time.

When children, however, have no access to culture and therefore cannot do imaginative work, they are at risk to relieve boredom with a little sadism here and there. If time passes and they still get no experience in imagining scenes not physically in front of their eyes, they will quite pathetically look for ways to break out of the boredom. They may, by the thousands, perhaps by the tens of thousands, amuse themselves by a mix of violent fantasizing (video games) and making other people cry. Their episodes of cruelty may get so thickly studded into their day's fabric that they conjoin. Then that child is at serious risk to become a sadist. Americans still heigh away from really acknowledging sadism in our being, but at least we know enough to call such people jerks.

A jerk, then—a repetitive gouger of others' well-being—can get a good start in the boredom that comes of being locked out of the imagination. In case this sounds melodramatic, bear in mind the clear pleasure that a cat gets from torturing a mouse whom she or he has bitten deeply enough so that it still cries and struggles to escape but can't. A smart cat can keep that going 20 minutes or longer.

Americans are extraordinarily bored now, even down to the children overeating in front the television or teenagers talking minimal nonsense to one another on their cell phones. And when any jungle mammal is bored it bites. Lab animals in captivity take to biting one another in a number of circumstances. One is boredom. At least someone else's pain is moderately interesting. Boredom leads small animals to scrapping, small children to gouging, and adolescent human beings to either or both physical and psychological vandalism.

## The Essential Element of any Stage-Development Philosophy is the Idea of Dynamics—Creatures Changing Because of Choices Made

People are not types. They are personalities whose feelings keep surging across from new perceptions to remembered perceptions and new feelings surging across and back from remembered feelings—whose concepts of what life is and what life should be keep shouting or quieting, changing or holding the same shores. The very dynamics of new thoughts change the brain. The very dynamics of new feelings replacing remembered feelings on a subject change the brain. What kinds of things do we decide when anyone tells other people "Let him who has ears to hear hear?" The speaker is saying that some people may not have been mentored or taught so that they have ears to hear complex ideas. Fire sirens yes, signs of core consciousness in people, no. What kinds of things do we decide to blow off? An absent-minded professor blows off where in the lot he or she left the car. A person brought up in the idea that the poor are always with us, and so are wars, blows off the idea of ethical improvement in the privileged classes.

## Dynamic Muscles, an Old Idea; Our Dynamic Brain a Newer Idea

Dozens of philosophers, once philosophy got interested in how people behave during their lives, as opposed to how the natural world got started, have written about the dynamic self-making properties of our upper cortex. The basic idea is not new. Recent neurology is now showing details of chemo-electric behavior of neurons and the amazing physiological properties of neurons which philosophers, the smart ones, suspected.

Blowing off ideas, as an example. Each time we blow off

a concept we further a neuronal habit—the most common neuronal habit being scorn for anything involving change. If we blow off the idea of the brain doing the work that street wisdom says is the work of the heart, then it is very hard to learn the brain's dynamics. Our brain is our engine of thought and imagination and altruism. Whatever we "blow off" shapes its core consciousness a little more. As it acts, the brain is making itself.

After the Empathic Stage-Development philosophy itself, an Afterword discusses some of the resistance human beings feel when confronted with an idea so systemic as stage-development theory. Any reader feeling offended or exasperated at this point in the reading could check the Afterword, out of curiosity about how the others may feel.

People are not types who show their character at some point early in life and then prove, later, to be more or less the type of person we took them for. The general notion of any stage theory is that people are genetically, chemically, and electrically given certain potentials for growth. Then, even before they are born, these biological potentials of ours live in an environment that has a lot of influence on them.

Once born, little human beings are tremendously specified by two more huge influences outside of themselves. The first one we have all heard of. Environment. Nurture. We know the old talk. Nature or nurture—which is it, that tells so much on a growing adult's personality? Old saws are usually true. That's why they are old saws. Still, it would be bad news in our personality growth if all that influenced us were a) electro-chemical presence in our skin and coming at it through our mothers' bloodstreams until birth, and then b) how our caretakers took care of us after that, and c) how just or unjust the governments of our caretakers were, since that would influence how well they could care for us.

Body parts changing as they act is not a new idea. The Use It or Lose It is the familiar principle about how exercising and habituating muscles to a certain amount and kind of activity changes those muscles. Personality, which has its places of rest and of firing and of neighboring in our brains, also is dynamic.

The brain as a dynamic part is not a new idea. Even before the 1990s' wonderful rush of neurological research and findings and philosophy, people had heard of "pathways" in the brain. In fact, "pathways" got bandied about as a word. There is little that our species fastens onto more proudly than new technical terms from some discipline we know little about. "Pathways," for example. Undergraduate education majors have used that word for a quarter-century. And what is a pathway? In the outside world, it is a place where people or other creatures have traveled so much it has grooved the countryside. Yes, of course. What's more engaging an idea is that if there is a discernable path, people and animals will follow it. That is, the pathway itself further habituates those who discern it into making use of it.

## The Most Unlevel Playing Field Since 19th Century Britain

Let's assume that Socrates and Solon—the great early Greek anti-jungle moralist[28] and philosophers and governors ever since, are right in saying that deliberate, conscious virtue gives life meaning more than simply living life beautifully. But who can do it?

Only the lucky.

1. We need luck in our parents.

   To get any kick out of anything so ethical as thinking about virtue, never mind practicing much of it, you need some good luck. First of all you need the good luck of your mother's not having used crack or meth while you were in her womb. Next,

---

[28] Solon introduced the idea of everyone being under the law. Greece had been ruled by its great families. Solon announced that might-makes-right was a ill-spirited idea. He insisted that each person had freedoms to be protected by law, and that no man was so rich he might be above the law. This was an extraordinarily new idea to most Greeks. In order to see the power of the idea, look at the pressure that rich families and tribes of families and boards of corporations put on a republic to get themselves prior consideration above the law. The law is the crux of keeping any republic from being frayed by the selfish rich.

you need fantastic good luck in having others help to develop your imagination. These others are first just caretakers, but later they are school teachers. They are traditionally aunts and uncles. No wonder so many 19th century novels about middle-class children have the visiting aunt or uncle whose coming—whose hilarity! whose wild remarks!—make a child burst into laughter. Whose visits have no practicality and a great deal of omnium invisibilium about them.

2. We need luck in our government.

Sadly, you need good luck in whatever government reigns in the land where you and your caretakers and your teachers live. The government must be kind enough to its citizenry, or at least to the citizens who are your parents or caretakers, so they were able to nurture you decently while your brain grew up to age 11 and past it. You have to get some education because the brain needs to get experience in being able to imagine a scene which is not the scene that your eyes, this very minute, are looking at. All unfair. The playing fields of the brain are unlevel. In fact, never has any playing field been less level in any period of history other than possibly the British Empire at the time of its Factory Act of August of 1833. It wasn't much of an act, either, but it did forbid the hiring of children under 9 years of age. It restricted work hours in children between age 9 and 13 to 48 hours a week. It restricted 13-to-18-year-old work hours to 69 hours a week. That is, to put it clearly, a conservative (Tory) employer might no longer make that kid work more than a 12-hour day, no matter how much he wanted to. Children under 13 were to have 2 hours' schooling each day.[29] Hundreds of conservatives howled in rebellion against that law! They wanted the slavery of those children so badly they made unspeakable

---

[29] The 1833 Factory Act was not the first but it was more merciful to children than the two that preceded it. Even so, it didn't speak to what happened to children in mines and in work other than textile factories.

complaints. Children brought up in the scruffy villages owned by those men had very bad luck.

Despite the horror of social history, we have to do a balancing act: we need to keep in mind how family culture, schools, and government can keep a young human being from developing the full imagination. At the same time, however, we need to exert the playfulness that adults can demonstrate to children. That playfulness and a sober sense of human meanness to children have to be kept together, both of them. This is not a feat that people pull off at the Happy Hour. It falls and stays in the hands of liberals.

So far we have listed the luck one must have. To make it clearer, let's look at an instance of failure—just as neurologists learned an awful lot about personality by looking at the skull of the workman, Gage, whose brain was stove through by his worktool in an explosion.

# A reminder of luck a child needs, since development of empathy so greatly, finally, depends on imagination.

1. Some chemical luck when the baby is in its mother
2. Some environmental (caretaking) luck in love received and freedom from criminality and from physical want.
3. Some luck in being mentored in imagining scenes that are not before your eyes at a given moment

Here is an example of environmental failure—what happened when a child had never heard playful stories told nor had whimsical conversation with any adults.

# Once upon a time a nanny goat went shopping

This story is known to professionals in elementary education in something like the way Gage's personality damage is known to neuroscientists.

A teacher reported this instance of a mid-20th-century education failure in the development of the imagination. The teacher herself was first bemused, then shocked, as she gradually realized what a child's symptoms meant.

She had told her 3rd grade class the story of the nanny goat and her 10 kids and the wolf. Her 10 kids were to dead bolt the door behind her and not let the wolf in under any circumstances. One child fidgeted, however, and finally said, "I don't get it." The teacher explained it was just a story, an entertainment, and you needn't "get" anything. All you have to do is imagine the wolf putting its chalked paw onto the window sill and speaking in a high squeaky voice to sound female, trying to talk the baby goats into taking him for their mother and letting him in.

The child remained standing before the teacher. "I just don't get it," she repeated. In writing up the incident, the teacher said that she believed that that child had heard no stories and had made up no stories but had only watched television and therefore had no dynamics of the imagination. The child could not imagine a goat or baby goats or a wolf.

Why should one rail if a child has an unexercised imagination? Why should a small publishing house create its own philosophy of stage development based on empathy?

Empathy is a cultural affect of human beings that is based nearly entirely on a developed imagination. If a child cannot imagine the kids and the nanny goat and the wolf, she will be unable to imagine people out of her physical vision field—let us say people living in other countries. If she cannot fathom playfulness itself, such as supposing a mother goat would fill up the wolf's belly with heavy stones and sew it up with the sewing kit that she happened to have ready at hand, that child will not only never have practiced making "a mental picture," but it will feel abnormal to her. She has never made a mental picture of anyone. Why do it now?

What is at stake with her lack of imagination is this question: what style of citizenship will she adopt for the rest of her life?

Let's take an immediate example. Say a child is read aloud to from *The Carpet Boy's Gift*,[30] a children's picture book based on the real life of a boy sold in bondage to a carpet manufacturer and who slaved there for years to pay off his family's debt. He escaped, stood up for the freedom and justice of the other children and was eventually both honored and murdered for his efforts. When receiving his Reebok Youth Action Award he said "I appeal to you that you stop people from using children as bonded laborers because the children need to use a pen rather than the instruments of child labor." So, let's say mom or dad read this story to their child of 8. It would take a little under an hour at most. Then let's say, OK that's where an hour of mental activity (making a mental image of the words) went for *that* child. Then, let's say another child watches a kidding TV sitcom or cartoon for a little under an hour. Now we can see the fantastic difference between what mental image the brain will make and never forget from the story versus the comfy joking and coarse drawing of the other. The one exercises the child's solemn insides. The other says, well here are some jokes, hey.

Empathy is not a raw emotion generated or processed in any way by our anterior cingulate or amygdalae or any other unconscious sites in the brain. It is a product of the neocortex's way of relaying thought and feeling around across the head. Empathy has nothing of the flee or fight or eat or sexually-molest kind of decision making that wells up from unconscious deposition in lower nuclei. Empathy is what is occurring when a human being perceives something in the outside world and then, within some tens or hundreds or thousands of milliseconds,[31] relates that new perception to previous perceptions further forward in the brain, these previous perceptions having been made on the same or a closely related subject—and finally makes some new value out of all the neurons' reports.

Now we return to the goat story and think about a post scriptum to the little girl's frustration with the teacher for saying

---
[30] Shea, Pegi Deitz, *The Carpet Boy's Gift*, Gardiner, ME, Tilbury House, Publishers, 2003.
[31] The neuroscientist Dr Antonio Damasio makes a fascinating observation about the speed of consciousness: it is much, much slower than the speed of neurons themselves. See *The Feeling of What Happens*, pages 126-127.

things about nanny goats and a wolf, when it makes no sense to her. That child's perception, her sensory perception as such, her early visual perception, may be perfectly all right. She perceives the classroom. She perceives the other children. She sees that they look alert, obviously having some feelings different from what she is feeling. They are doing a brain process that she has never done: they are making a mental picture of something that is not before their eyes. She doesn't know that, but she feels frustrated because those other children look intense—we would say focused—since they are exercising higher-level consciousness upon an invisible subject. [Goats and wolf, that is, being invisible to them.] She sees enjoyment, not tedium, in their faces. Yet she herself feels tedium.

What the child is up against is right now, in the classroom, her feelings of being left out of something clearly enjoyable to the others. What she is at risk to be up against for the rest of her life is not being invited to imagine anything that is not in her actual visual field. Well, so what? A two-year-old gets awfully cross when Mom and Dad play so differently with the little wooden chess pieces they touch, move, touch again, from how he, the two-year-old, plays with his little figures. He can see how they watch each other's moves and they make exclamations. They shout things like "Mate, I think!" and the other one looks rueful. A two-year-old learns to suffer about the greater joy of adults. But a thirty-year-old?

Two decades have passed since the nanny goat story. That little girl is now twenty-eight years old. Let us say she is a citizen of a nation. Most of us are. Let us say her country decides to bomb people in another country. She has not made a mental picture of how it is for people in that country. Why should she do so? If you suggest she imagine some country far away like that, perhaps a country with a smashed infrastructure so far as medical-service delivery or safe drinking water are concerned, she suspects she will feel more uneasy, not less uneasy, if she does so. She can see a more intense game in your face. She is resistant to painful image making but she is socialized at an intricate level: she can see that you want her to feel pain that is nothing to do with herself or any one of her friends.

Peace activists of the past half-century have a way of rushing up to adults like her and saying, "Don't you see? Don't you see? Some of those people are little children, even!"

What she very likely will "see" will be what she saw at age eight when the teacher described the wolf who had whitened his paws and chalked his throat. She will see that the others, twenty years ago the other kids in that class, now this peace activist, are having a better time than she is.

She is not stupid. As a matter of fact, people with ill-developed imaginations are often remarkably socialized to what the others seem to be doing. They look for more signals from others in the room than imaginative people do. They often have an unerring sense of who's having more fun than they themselves. They feel cross about it. Damned if they're going to join some oddball protest on behalf of people in some godforsaken place!

We believe that the liveliest way for someone to get the hang of empathic stage-development is to read the theory, argument by argument, and try each in turn against your own life. This is an utterly 100% anecdotal approach. By the way, if someone grins at you when you say you are testing an empathic stage theory against your own recalled past, you can say, "Right! All very anecdotal! All very theoretical! No, you're right. I haven't any proof there's anything in it! It's just like Einstein's $E=mc^2$ for all the years before lesser scientists came up with celestial tools for measuring his ideas. Math is thought and thought always comes before measurement!"

Stave them off with that. If that won't hold back a flood of scorn, you can point out Socrates's remark about the unexamined life's not being worth living. He was putting stage-development philosophy briefly into the negative. The personally examined life is wonderfully, wonderfully, worth living. It is the story that we tell ourselves all over our cortices. Occasionally we learn to change from it. Occasionally no particular ethical improvement comes out of it.

An example: My own first failure in empathic stage development took place when I was four. I was perfectly conscious of the disgrace involved. I didn't know any theories for the sin but I knew moral shortfall when I saw people pointing to it. I had not moved from Stage 1 to Stage 2 whereas other members of my Kindergarten class had made the cut. I flunked Kindergarten. My teacher and my mother stood in that arrogant sky-scraper posture of adults and richly betrayed me back and forth in a conversation that sounded as though it were perfectly agreeable to them. My teacher distinctly said, "She is just a little Princess still. She still doesn't see any world outside." True enough, I expect. My mother seemed to be agreeing with her. What I heard was the disloyalty if it! You'd think—I remember thinking this at that time—that one's own mother could have stood up for her child. I knew it was wrong to be a self-absorbed little princess, but I also deeply felt that the disloyalty of those two adults was criminal, and criminality felt more consequential to me than self-absorption.

That is a childish example to illustrate two psychological dynamics that are natural if not admirable in little kids which, in adults, make people behave badly in groups. First, self-absorption which is, empathically speaking, Stage 1. And second, in Stage 1 or even worse in the tribal stage, Stage 2, loyalty has stronger cachet than wrong-doing.

This is worth thinking about because in our species, there are so many billions of adults who happen to be stuck in Tribal Stage 2. No matter whether they are blithe family members or sore-headed family members, or blithe church members or sore-headed church members. All they do is defend their group. If their family, tribe, or church advocates assault on far distant peoples they will feel little or no pity for those far-distant peoples. That is what it means to be stuck in Stage 2. That is the stage that flies into outrage more about loyalty than about any other group feeling.

All this to illustrate how a personal anecdote is useful in

reading and thinking about empathic stage development. You can experiment in some punctilious navel watching! That is, you might ask yourself: what scene do I remember when I was in stage 3? What do I remember about being in stage 4? And so on. Even J.D. Salinger's wonderful protagonist, Holden Caulfield, who spoke throughout *Catcher in the Rye* in a voice of solid stage 5—committing himself to his own self-made philosophy without reference to "authority" and without reference to "peers"—even he must have been a stage one-er or stage two-er or stage 3 or 4 fellow back when.

We suggest reading the whole stage-development outline in a deliberately self-oriented way. We suggest reading it lightly if you can. Stage-development philosophy is not grim. It is a thousand times more cheering and usually more exacting of truth than stereotyping yourself or anyone else is.

It wants attention. A funny almost universal weakness of human beings is attributing adult insights or skills to oneself at an earlier age than one had such insights or skills. Authors are much given to this. "At eight I wrote my first novel," they say to interviewers whereas the truth was they wrote it at ten, not eight, and the novel was four pages long. They don't always mean to lie but the memory of their first little brown desk is so clear.

It doesn't matter so much if egoists lie about incidental aesthetic achievements. It doesn't even matter much if Tibetan Buddhists lie about their meditations—saying how refreshed they always feel after meditation even though they slept through 25 minutes of the 30-minute meditation. It does matter to ourselves if we are trying seriously to understand psycho-ethical growth if we can't make ourselves do the crusty business of telling the truth. Lawrence Kohlberg observed that people describing to others one or another of the upper moral-reasoning stages would take up a noticeably petulant tone. He suggested that the speaker's irritation came of the irritation human beings tend to have when they are in the presence of moral taste—or even aesthetic taste—that is *more developed than their own*. The little girl unable to get a kick out of a story about a nanny goat and

10 kids feels cross at the children who do imagine it and enjoy it. A stage four person—someone who takes their most serious guidance from civic or military authorities—rather hates a Stage 5 person: that is likely because that obedient follower feels the superiority of doing one's own thinking. Soon that Stage 4 person will be doing more and more evaluation himself or herself. For now, beginning to weigh dutiful obedience against individual ethics, the Stage 4 person is beginning to suffer.

A study aid: don't plan to discuss your own development with anyone. It is easier not to lie to yourself about what you were really aware of when, how far back, if you plan not to tell anyone about this meditation you are doing. The temptation is to confess, with a caveat about not wanting to boast, that so far as you can tell, looking back, you always were kind of Stage 5.

## Here, then, is our Stage-Development Theory for the empathic imagination

1. ONESELF.
   Feeling only one's own wants and satisfactions. You can't expect a nursing baby to relinquish the breast for a quarter-hour because a third-world child is starving and needs it. A baby hasn't got and cannot practice the idea of constraint. Nor should a baby practice non-expression of its needs. Self-serving is fine for a baby.[32] When a young adult is stuck in Stage 1 we feel gloomy indeed. Words like sociopath come to mind.

   <u>A cultural note about Stage 1</u>

   Babies are usually wonderfully "relational," as the feminists are still fond of saying. They love their caretakers. In fact, they are in psychological trouble if they don't. Most of us have seen some of the vast literature about attachment failure in children. It is hard work that the brain is doing for a young child.

---

[32] Bear in mind Stage 6 people feel sad, outraged, etc. when they hear of children being tortured or killed in foreign lands. Babies don't start Amnesty International.

2. ONE'S TRIBE.
Respecting only one's own tribe or family, or the family's choice of church, and others who like you respect only their families, their families' churches, and so forth. There is often a hit-or-miss tolerance among tribal-stage people. Fundamentalists of any religion, for example, feel an inchoate but genuine respect for fundamentalists of some other religion. Perhaps, even when one solidly subscribes to we-good, they-less-good at the tribal stage, one can and often does "identify with" others at the same stage. Play therapists report very small children weeping when they see other children weeping. Their reports suggest that those children are not especially sympathizing with the child they see weeping but that they see themselves in the other children. It isn't empathy. It is "identifying with." They sympathize with their projected selves in the other children. Rather than disrespecting that dynamic we should realize that identifying with anyone or anything other than oneself is a sound act of the imagination. It is an early step on one of the pilgrimages going on in the human cortex.

A cultural note about Tribal Stage 2:

This is the stage in which the greatest number of human beings get stuck all of their working lives because of money. Business, roughly speaking, and definitely foreign-policy making, do not operate on the basis of empathy except in the sense of indentifying psychological weaknesses in one's rivals or enemies.[33] Businesses, as do training squads in the army, want their cadres made up of Tribal Stage 2 people—that is, loyalists who defer to authorities on top and who are unswervingly loyal to compeers. Stage 2 people don't admire inventiveness so much

---

[33] There are three great industrial psychologists, to use that expression to mean people who use psychology not to help others but in order to manipulate those others either to buy one's produce or to yield up rights or real property to one's own side. Sun Tzu, Machiavelli, and Clausewitz. What these men talk about is imaginative attention paid to one's mark or to an enemy, but it is quite opposite to empathy. Q.V. discussed on pages 14 & 76

as their public relations would suggest. Businesses and drill instructors don't want invention: they want a public parallel to family loyalty:

> "[Most companies], even those considered 'visionary,' emphasize mechanisms of social control rather than innovation. They recognize the power of clear goals, worker participation, consistent feedback, a cohesive work force, and a reward system that underscores desired behaviors and values. In fact, the 'spark' that many companies are likely to ignite is not innovation or risk taking, but rather loyalty and commitment to the company. They attempt to create a cult-like culture involving passion and excitement. Through this path they may achieve productivity and high morale, but at the same time can thwart creativity, innovation, and an ability 'to respond readily to change.'" [34]

3. TAKING OUR CUES AND OUR GUIDANCE FROM PEERS
In this stage we love our peer group. We want to do what we see them doing. Stage 3 is a perfectly functional stage for pre-teens and teens. Teenaged people don't want to dress the way their parents think they should. They want to be like the kids of a crowd they have assessed as "popular." Probably most human beings stay in Stage 3 or 4 all of their lives. In this stage nearly all influence on how the brain thinks comes from the culture and most people never get an education that helps free the organism from conventionality. People get stuck in stage 3 because no one near by is in any better stage. In rural towns, for example, throughout history, people look to see what the others are thinking and doing.

C.S. Lewis's sharp-edged essay, "The Inner Ring," describes stage 3 workings that happen to be cruel. All mammals do cruel obeisance to pecking-order thinking. We call it social climbing and class snobbery when it is homo sapiens. Social

---
[34] Charlan Jeanne Nemeth, "Managing Innovation: When Less is More," California Management Review, Vol. 40, No. 1, Fall, 1997

climbing can be such a major passion that it can overwhelm other passions, the way gambling does. Its victims sell out people and property, to feed the passion. That brings about ugly cruelties inside families and between families and in small civic settings, but it feeds a further limbic-system passion that is part of our mammal heritage—C.S. Lewis focused on this—it is the mammal enjoyment of hurting others. In Lewis's view, belonging to the better club gives you the sharp added flavor. Others were wounded because they were not asked, and you get to regard their wounds like driving past an auto wreck when it is still fresh. Note the exquisite cruelty of 11- and 12-year-old girls at slumber parties in how they treat the "ugly" girl whom they have deliberately invited for just this purpose.

4. THE STAGE IN WHICH WE NOT ONLY TAKE GUIDANCE FROM LEADERS BUT WE ARE AT RISK TO ADORE THEM. Stage 4 people make wonderful British servants. Stage 4 people follow the Adolf Hitlers of the world, probably for the reasons given by the psychoanalyst Alice Miller in her book about the psychology of those Germans who were charismatized by Hitler.[35]

The greatest novel whose major theme, the central subject, is stage 4 personality is *Remains of the Day*. One of its two Stage 4 protagonists is a privileged country-house-owning Englishman who is wistful about Nazism in Germany. The other is his butler. Kazuo Ishiguro's book is intricately done. Usually, psychological professionals are the most astute about Stage 4. In this case, an author is.

A cultural note about both Stage 3 and Stage 4

We want to offer this side comment about the two very conventional stages, 3 and 4. In 3 people still love whomever

---

[35] Alice Miller, *For Your Own Good*

they loved in Stage 2—their caretakers, their parents, their tribal big shots—but now they are torn. They love those tribal leaders but they want to take at least 50% of their guidance from their peers. They are often quite fascinated by their peers. People in Stage 4—usually called an authoritarian stage—still love parents and also their peers but now have added a new feeling into their consciousness: it is conscientious allegiance to leaders. That is, the new emotion involved has a moral feeling about it. One feels a rightness about obeying leaders. One feels a wrongness if one refuses to obey leaders. And these leaders govern more than just the household. They govern civic organizations, the largest of which is the national government.

Stage 3 and Stage 4 are jagged, wildly careening stages. A good deal is written about adolescents' chemical imbalances, which are necessarily present. Less is written about the outer contradictions that an adolescent must resolve in some way. Already, let us say, the adolescent loves his or her parents and other tribal entities. Already, however, he or she loves and admires peers. The peers lead in directions that bring down ire from the parents. The parents lead in directions that catapult the young people's peers into scorn.

Now let's add in the dynamics of Stage 4—love of authority—a conscientious attitude toward government. What this does for an adolescent is expose him or her to three sets of thoroughly conflicting ethics:

1. Right and wrong as seen in the more or less "old time religion" of parental love,
2. Cool versus weird as seen in the peer group, and finally,
3. A call for obedience from one's own country. Since one's country designs its recruiting promotion to please and charm non-judgmental citizenry, the government can effectively use the simplest, most sensational of the media to encourage spontaneous joining up, to hype up the moment so a young person scarcely has time for building his or her own opinion about government's policies.

*The New Yorker* offers in its July 4, 2005, issue a very great piece of private-individual-person-sized American history called "The Home Front," by George Packer. Packer shows us a heartbreaking picture of a soldier's father, Chris Forsheiser. What Packer keeps a respectful focus on is the way Chris Frosheiser, a liberal with patriotic feeling, tries to make sense of the United States assault on Iraq. What is psychologically engaging is that Chris Frosheiser believes in turning issues over in his mind. He is a thoughtful man. [And the essay's author, George Packer, has the vision and generosity to stick with Frosheiser. They had a correspondence after Packer's talks with the man.] Some people put their souls to work a lot more industriously than other people. Kurt Frosheiser's grieving father is one of them. Most people, however, do not try to grasp which psychological dynamics may be dictating what our *leaders* do. They should. What drives rightist American military leadership should be a subject of study for Chris Frosheiser. Our dimwitted culture, however, does not teach studying one's *leaders* in order to see if there are some reasons for evil to prevail that we need to know about. Often the real casus belli is in some psychological snarl of the *leader*.

5. DOING ONE'S OWN JUDGMENTS ABOUT THE WORLD
   A Stage-5 person stands apart from family, society, and all others in his or her feelings about how human beings treat one another. In this stage one can see objects and people that do not actually stand before one's eyes. The imagination is complete—well, as we ever see imagination as complete. A perfect example of a literary plea for people to try to think critically like a Stage 5 person was Virginia Woolf's *Three Guineas*.

Woolf gave us this timeless scene: she asks us to imagine ourselves sitting at a long oval table of the kind people sit at who are magnates in their field. Today (she says) the field we are dealing with is war, so the magnates sitting all along both sides and at the end of the table are staff-grade officers—majors and higher. They wear the British khaki and red lapels. (Virginia Woolf was British.) They are highly decorated so our eyes see before us pretty ribbons and bright metal on these men's chests. They are planning a worthy war of some sort, she tells us. Then Woolf says that we need *not* to see those solemn and handsome faces, those khaki chests with their insignia of honor. We need, instead, to make a mental picture of dead soldiers. Those dead soldiers are very important to the war being planned.

When I first read that suggestion of Woolf's I recalled a cover of *Life*, which just before and during World War II was a brilliant news presence in American houses. This particular cover was a full-sized black and white photograph showing two or three Americans, soldiers or marines, whose units had attacked a beach. These particular young men were among those killed. Now, because the burial detail hadn't reached them yet, their bodies had taken at least one, perhaps two incoming and ebbing tides. Wave action had scoured sand from the sea's side of these men's bodies, and deltaed them gently on the land side. One or two tides had begun smoothing the angles of their arms and legs. Those bodies had become foils for the sea. I do not revere Virginia Woolf's gem-laden style much, but I will never forget her as a moralist calling us to Stage 5—to see whatever sadness lies behind the gleam of whatever medals we admire.

6. IMAGINING WHO AND WHAT LIE FARTHER FROM HOME THAN I WILL EVER VISIT, AND HOPING THEY GET A FAIR SHAKE.

Stage 6 is a rare stage because it requires such unsparing use of the re-entry consciousness in the brain. Reentry, put very simply, is the thought-and-feeling process of the millions of neurons in our neocortex as they carry forward from the sense centers at the back and sides of our heads the latest news to the contemplation centers where we human beings make our comment on what's coming down. The process involves thousands of groupings of neurons with different memories conferring first, so to speak, among neighbors, and then conferring with neurons from all across the 6-layered cortex, not to mention picking up some feeling remarks from the basal, unconscious centers below. This is we, human beings, thinking at our least self-serving. This is we at our most critical.

I have not yet arrived at Stage 6 but I have three or four times seen people who looked like Stage six-ers all right. Here is how to spot one. They know that if mercy and justice are what they crave for themselves then mercy and justice are what other creatures want, too. They restrain themselves from drinking the planet's last clear water.

John Donne has a paragraph lovingly quoted by both good people and scoundrels. In it he makes a succinct doctrine for Stage 6. We are each part of the Continent, so if a clod be washed away it is as if a promontory were washed away. Therefore we needn't send to find for whom the bell tolls, Donne tells us, because all tolling is always for all of us.

When we hear that paragraph, we wish we were at Stage 6. Donne was nothing if not summoning. However ratty our occasional behaviors, human beings do have this endearing quality: we suppose that Stage 6 is as good as homo sapiens can do, and at our best, we want to go there.

## An Afterword: Getting Over Resisting Helpful Theories About Empathy

At Bly & Loveland Press we have been surprised by wide resistance to moral stage-development philosophy. We were not surprised that literary professionals were either disgusted, or bored by the idea, but we are disappointed that professional social workers fail to snatch for it. The idea that a person treated respectfully and empathically would ratchet their personalities by degrees from self-absorption to altruism should be meat and potatoes to professional social workers.

In the event, however, social workers have by and large paid no thanks to Lawrence Kohlberg's writing about moral stage development, nor to others. People interested in Rogers's therapy-interviewing style have not been interested in his work as a stage-developmental philosopher.

English departments don't pretend to be "helping professionals" in any sense of the word so no one should be disappointed that professors and instructors don't generally know whether or how to teach "Why I Write," Orwell's essay in which he endearingly tells us about the *four stages* in his own development as a writer. The first two were stages of greed and adolescent beauty-worship. If young creative-writing-program customers were introduced to "Why I Write" they might save themselves years of being blithely unconscious of how passionate greed for success drives writers to write what Orwell called *mostly humbug*—we would get through all that much more quickly. Lecturers and instructors and professors who cotton to "Politics and the English Language," not to mention those who wholeheartedly praise *The Road to Wigan Pier* and *Down and Out in Paris and London,* seldom give the time of day to George Orwell's very edifying four stages of psychology. Literature is often an exquisite hobby, however, not a teaching tool at all. Perhaps psychology and literature, which seem so amazingly close and even part and parcel of one another are, in the hands of thousands of pedagogists, actually inimical.

What is such refusal to see inner change about? Perhaps people naturally despise psychological dynamics. Perhaps they despise the idea that a brain changes whenever it acts actively on any of its concepts.

A glittering example of lay people resisting anything psychological even when it clearly would benefit the professionals in their own field is the Prussian rejection, for over a century, of the very idea of industrial psychology as it could be applied to soldiery. Carl von Clausewitz, an enlisted man eventually made a commissioned officer, wrote that military people should study the enemy's wants, needs, skills, weaknesses. His *On War* received the great classical response that professional enclaves of fools lavish upon any individual genius: *scorn*. See the note on page 14.

## A List of Possible Reasons for Being Unwilling to Take Empathic Stage Development Theory Seriously

1. No one I know of equal or superior status to mine talks about empathic or any other stage-development theory. I would risk the perhaps still loyal but unmistakable scorn of my peers and colleagues if I began to think and talk about dynamic explanations of empathy and altruism in the brain.

2. Why should I have to suffer the pain of new thinking that might push me toward change of myself? All my life I and those I know have considered people to be certain types, to have certain kinds of character—stable personalities. We know all we want to know of what genes specify for in cells or in potential development of cells. Systems enthusiasts are, let's face it, exasperating.

3. I intend to stay clear of any line of thought that suggests psychological progressions toward altruism. Nor do I want to recognize and oppose whatever psychological dynamics *discourage* altruistic development. I have taken pains to learn

to see the bright side of things, a point of view I grant is easier if one regards only one side of an issue. But people make such a holy cow of *truth*! But truth isn't always the right answer. Being able to live in some balance and without constant mood swings—sometimes that's a lot more sensible a goal than truth-seeking.

4. I am of the opinion—and I have a right to my opinion!—that the thinking of stage developmentalists is detrimental to the principles I and my people have chosen to live by.

5. I don't mind scorn in its rightful place. Thank goodness we are now civilized, most of us. We are a long way from the book burnings of May and June of 1933. Still, that doesn't mean we have to tolerate fancy psychobabble coming at us from the outside. What's wrong with practicing one's profession or enjoying one's hobby without connecting it to everything in the world? I like things to be discreet from one another, not all the time connected, and worse, in some sort of brain flux.

Bly & Loveland Press grew out of a Minnesota School Social Workers' Association committee that published activist pamphlets. MSSWA generously gave budget and volunteers to work up two pamphlets showing how empathy is related to mercy towards others even if you don't know those others. The pamphlets pointed to corporations whose money-making styles do damage to how young people develop their imaginations.

In those pamphlets[36] and in the first two books of our Press[37] we tried to show, again and again, how everything ethical depends on human beings' being able to imagine the plight of others. Again and again we noticed how people generally

---

[36] MSSWA Pamphlet #1 was called *A Letter to Three Corporations who Sponsor Extraordinarily Violent TV Programs: Kellogg, Sony Corporation of America, AOL Time Warner.* MSSWA Pamphlet #2 was called *A New Psychology for the Privileged Perpetrator.*

[37] *Three Readings for Republicans and Democrats* and *Stopping the Gallop to Empire.* These books are available from Bly & Loveland Press, 5537 Zenith Avenue South, Edina, MN 55410

resisted these ideas.

Perhaps it is that people are ethically slothful. Perhaps it is that moralists are always, eternally, *on* about something. They never relax. Relaxation must not be so dear to them as it is to people who never have gotten the pleasant habit of making connections between what looks on the surface like meaningless fragments of one perception and some old remembered concepts or other.

Or perhaps, like primitives, most of us actually hate the individual, contemplative voice. No matter that those who think for themselves and who want justice and mercy on behalf of everyone are the people who make the human advances. Primitive cultures are called primitive for good reason: they seriously fear individuality.

Here is a less annoying parallel. If our working lives in society are anything like a huge ship, then some people choose or are chosen to spot previously unseen things, namely to take watches in the crow's nest, squinting in all the directions.

Others have their equally honorable and exhausting work at the ship's computers or engines. Gorgeous idealists of the 19th century, William Morris or Bronson Alcott or John Ruskin, for example, had for their central common interest the goal of getting the inactive privileged of society to see the good of *manual* work and to do it, and getting them to help traditional manual workers join "the General Dance." The idea was if we are all potentially brothers and sisters but are behaving the way we behave, somebody has to quit doing what they are doing and behave more altruistically.

In our century we look at the other side of it. Idealists of the 21st century should try to make it possible for more of the manual workers, the non-privileged of society, to do imaginative work. Say there is a rough country school class full of ordinary-looking children: which is the one that will be Abraham Lincoln?

If "the General Dance" is all of the mind's delights our species has evolved any taste for so far, which is the one of those children who will "get it," but even better, will feel exercised to help others join the General Dance? Since we can't know, we can't tell from the mended overalls, we had better educate them all for empathic stages 5 and 6.

Let's waste a moment and ask ourselves a surprisingly searching question: how many times, if even once, were we told by those who were our caretakers or our teachers, *not* to be practical? Wolves teach their cubs practicality, of course. Practicality is not good enough for homo sapiens. We have come too far and we've barely started. We sometimes regress fast as a cat, too. All of a sudden someone is burning books again!

It is hard for us to trust that each brain, left in calmness, but guided in imagination, will tear along collecting itself to make a philosophy to present to the boss (its organism).

Most of us don't know any neurologists. And if we undertook psychotherapy for self-educative purpose, in all humility, we may have done it with a dumbbell. Too bad.

The bright neurologists and the bright therapists are already telling us: neurons like those in the heads of Socrates, Virginia Woolf, George Orwell, John Rawls, I.F. Stone, Senator Robert Byrd, and Bill Moyers, are firing and firing in great bands inside our heads, too.

# Appendix
## Table of Contents

From the Contitution of the United States     83
    Article III with Amendment XI
    Article II Section. 2

United State Senate Committee on the Judiciary     85
[As of June, 2005]

U.S. Senate Confirms Alberto Gonzales 60 to 36     87
    Senatorial No votes on the confirmation of Alberto Gonzales
    as the U.S. Attorney General
    6 Senate Democrats who voted *YES* to Gonzales confirmation

A Little Information About Marbury v Madison, 1804     89
    Supreme Court declared an act of Congress invalid
    Supreme Court declared a section of the Judiciary Act of 1789 unconstitutional
    Marbury v Madison is generally considered the decision that made the United
    States Supreme Court the arbiter of what was constitutional and what wasn't—
    that is, the Supreme Court now had the right of judicial review in any law
    passed by the Congress and signed by the President.

Supreme Court Nominations Not Confirmed by the Senate
from 1793 to the Present     91

An Unusual Insight Into Thomas Jefferson's Fear
of the Federal Judiiciary     93

A Very Small Bibliography to Introduce People to
some Up-to-Date Neurological Thinking     95

## Contitution for the United States of America

### Article III

Section. 1. The judicial Power of the United States shall be vested in one supreme Court, and in such inferior Courts as the Congress may from time to time ordain and establish. The Judges, both of the supreme and inferior Courts, shall hold their Offices during good Behaviour, and shall, at stated Times, receive for their Services a Compensation, which shall not be diminished during their Continuance in Office.

Section. 2. The judicial Power shall extend to all Cases, in Law and Equity, arising under this Constitution, the Laws of the United States, and Treaties made, or which shall be made, under their Authority;—to all Cases affecting Ambassadors, and other public Ministers and Consuls;—to all Cases of admiralty and maritime Jurisdiction;—to Controversies to which the United States shall be a Party;—to Controversies between two or more States;—between a State and Citizens of another State [Modified by Amendment XI];—between Citizens of Different States;—between Citizens of the same State claiming Lands under Grants of different States, and between a State, or the Citizens thereof, and foreign States, Citizens or Subjects.

In all cases affecting Ambassadors, other public Ministers and Consuls, and those in which a State shall be Party, the supreme Court shall have original Jurisdiction. In all other Cases before mentioned, the supreme Court shall have appellate Jurisdiction, both as to Law and Fact, with such Exceptions, and under such Regulations as the Congress shall make.

The Trial of all Crimes, except in Cases of Impeachment, shall be by Jury; and such Trial shall be held in the State where the said Crimes shall have been committed; but when not committed within any State, the Trial shall be at such Place or Places as the Congress may by Law have directed.

Section. 3. Treason against the United States shall consist only in levying War against them, or in adhering to their Enemies, giving them Aid and Comfort. No Person shall be convicted of Treason unless on the Testimony of two Witnesses to the same overt Act, or on Confession in open Court.

The Congress shall have Power to declare the Punishment of Treason, but no Attainder of Treason shall work Corruption of Blood, or Forfeiture except during the Life of the Person attainted.

## AMENDMENT XI
*Passed by Congress March 4, 1794. Ratified February 7, 1795.*

**Note**: Article III, section 2, of the Constitution was modified by amendment 11.

The Judicial power of the United States shall not be construed to extend to any suit in law or equity, commenced or prosecuted against one of the United States by Citizens of another State, or by Citizens or Subjects of any Foreign State.

## ARTICLE II

Section. 2. [paragraph 2, The president] shall have Power, by and with the Advice and Consent of the Senate, to make Treaties, provided two thirds of the Senators present concur; and he shall nominate, and by and with the Advice and Consent of the Senate, shall appoint Ambassadors, other public Ministers and Consuls, Judges of the supreme Court, and all other Officers of the United States, whose Appointments are not herein otherwise provided for, and which shall be established by Law: but the Congress may by Law vest the Appointment of such inferior Officers, as they think proper, in the President alone, in the Courts of Law, or in the Heads of Departments.

## United States Senate
## Committee on the Judiciary

**Arlen Specter**
CHAIRMAN, PENNSYLVANIA

**Orrin G. Hatch**
Utah

**Charles E. Grassley**
Iowa

**Jon Kyl**
Arizona

**Mike DeWine**
Ohio

**Jeff Sessions**
Alabama

**Lindsey Graham**
South Carolina

**John Cornyn**
Texas

**Sam Brownback**
Kansas

**Tom Coburn**
Oklahoma

**Patrick J. Leahy**
Ranking Democratic Member,
Vermont

**Edward M. Kennedy**
Massachusetts

**Joseph R. Biden, Jr.**
Delaware

**Herbert Kohl**
Wisconsin

**Dianne Feinstein**
California

**Russell D. Feingold**
Wisconsin

**Charles E. Schumer**
New York

**Richard J. Durbin**
Illinois

## Senate Confirmation of Alberto Gonzales as U.S. Attorney General

On February 2, 2005, the Senate voted 60-36 to confirm President Bush's nomination of Alberto Gonzales as U. S. Attorney General. In the last seven decades only Attorney General John Ashcroft received more no votes on his confirmation.

The thirty-six no votes were cast by 35 Democrats and one Independent. They are as follows:

| | | |
|---|---|---|
| Akaka (HI) | Dorgan (ND) | Levin (MI) |
| Bayh (IN) | Durbin (IL)* | Lincoln (AR) |
| Biden (DE)* | Feingold (WI)* | Mikulski (MD) |
| Bingaman (NM) | Feinstein (CA)* | Murray (WA) |
| Boxer (CA) | Harkin (IA) | Obama (IL) |
| Byrd (WV) | Jeffords (VT)** | Reed (RI) |
| Cantwell (WA) | Johnson (SD) | Reid (NV) |
| Carper (DE) | Kennedy (MA)* | Rockefeller (WV) |
| Clinton (NY) | Kerry (MA) | Sarbanes (MD) |
| Corzine (NJ) | Kohl (WI)* | Schumer (NY)* |
| Dayton (MN) | Lautenberg (NJ) | Stabenow (MI) |
| Dodd (CT) | Leahy (VT)* | Wyden (OR) |

\* members of the Senate Judiciary Committee
\*\* Independent

No Republicans voted against the nomination. Six Democrats voted to confirm Gonzales. They are:

| | |
|---|---|
| Landrieu (LA) | Nelson, Bill (FL) |
| Liberman (CT) | Pryor (AK) |
| Nelson, Ben (NE) | Salazar (CO) |

The Senate Judiciary Committee voted 10-8 along strict party lines to send the nomination to the floor of the Senate. Many issues were alarming but most particularly Gonzales's advice on administering torture to prisoners of war and his memo declaring provisions of the Geneva Convention "quaint and obsolete."

## Marbury v. Madison 1804

### The Case That Made All the Difference
### The Supreme Court Claimed the Power to Nullify Previously Made Legislation By Declaring it Unconstitutional

In 1804 a judicial decision was handed down by the U. S. Supreme Court in a case known as Marbury v. Madison. The case was started because President Jefferson did not like one of the appointments made by his predecessor in the Presidency, John Adams. The appointment, made in the last few hours of Adams' administration in 1801, elevated a man named William Marbury to the position of justice of the peace. Jefferson asked his Secretary of State, James Madison, to dismiss Marbury, and Marbury sued the government in the person of Madison so that he might be reinstated in his job. The case went all the way to the U.S. Supreme Court, which dismissed Marbury's suit, stating that the court lacked jurisdiction in the case. More importantly, the Supreme Court declared that a section of the Judiciary Act of 1789 was unconstitutional. This was the first time that the Supreme Court declared an act of Congress invalid, which opened a new role for the court, eventually gaining for it an important place as the third, co-equal branch of government, along with the Congress and the Executive.

The critical importance of Marbury is the assumption of several powers by the Supreme Court. One was the authority to declare acts of Congress, and by implication acts of the president, unconstitutional if they exceeded the powers granted by the Constitution. But even more important, the Court became the arbiter of the Constitution, the final authority on what the document meant. As such, the Supreme Court became in fact as well as in theory an equal partner in government, and it has played that role ever since.

The Court would not declare another act of Congress unconstitutional until 1857, and it has used that power sparingly. But through its role as arbiter of the Constitution, it has, especially in the twentieth century, been the chief agency for the expansion of individual rights.

from *Basic Readings in US Democracy*, by Melvin I. Urofsky, Professor of Constitutional History, Virginia Commonwealth University, Richmond, Virginia

## Supreme Court Nominations Not Confirmed by the Senate

In the more than two centuries from 1789 to 1996, the Senate has rejected Supreme Court nominees twenty-eight times. One nominee, Edward King, twice failed to win Senate confirmation. A dozen have been rejected outright, and the remainder have been withdrawn or allowed to lapse when Senate rejection seemed imminent. Three were renominated later and confirmed. Following is the complete list of nominees failing to receive confirmation:

| Nominee | President | Date of Nomination | Senate Action | Date of Senate Action |
|---|---|---|---|---|
| William Paterson | Washington | February 27, 1793 | Withdrawn [1] | |
| John Rutledge [2] | Washington | July 1, 1795 | Rejected (10-14) | December 15, 1795 |
| Alexander Wolcott | Madison | February 4, 1811 | Rejected (9-24) | February 13, 1811 |
| John J. Crittenden | John Quincy Adams | December 17, 1828 | Postponed | February 12, 1829 |
| Roger Brooke Taney | Jackson | January 15, 1835 | Postponed (24-21) [3] | March 3, 1835 |
| John C. Spencer | Tyler | January 9, 1844 | Rejected (21-26) | January 31, 1844 |
| Reuben H. Walworth | Tyler | March 13, 1844 | Withdrawn | |
| Edward King | Tyler | June 5, 1844 | Postponed | June 15, 1844 |
| Edward King | Tyler | December 4, 1844 | Withdrawn | |
| John M. Read | Tyler | February 7, 1845 | Not acted upon | |
| George W. Woodward | Polk | December 23, 1845 | Rejected (20-29) | January 22, 1846 |
| Edward A. Bradford | Fillmore | August 16, 1852 | Not acted upon | |
| George E. Badger | Fillmore | January 10, 1853 | Postponed | February 11, 1853 |
| William C. Micou | Fillmore | February 24, 1853 | Not acted upon | |
| Jeremiah S. Black | Buchanan | February 5, 1861 | Rejected (25-26) | February 21, 1861 |
| Henry Stanbery | Andrew Johnson | April 16, 1866 | Not acted upon | |
| Ebenezer R. Hoar | Grant | December 15, 1869 | Rejected (24-33) | February 3, 1870 |
| George H. Williams [2] | Grant | December 1, 1873 | Withdrawn | |
| Caleb Cushing [2] | Grant | January 9, 1874 | Withdrawn | |
| Stanley Matthews | Hayes | January 26, 1881 | Not acted upon [1] | |
| William B. Hornblower | Cleveland | September 19, 1893 | Rejected (24-30) | January 15, 1894 |
| Wheeler H. Peckham | Cleveland | January 22, 1894 | Rejected (32-41) | February 16, 1894 |
| John J. Parker | Hoover | March 21, 1930 | Rejected (39-41) | May 7, 1930 |
| Abe Fortas [2] | Lyndon Johnson | June 26, 1968 | Withdrawn | |
| Homer Thornberry | Lyndon Johnson | June 26, 1968 | Not acted upon | |
| Clement F. Haynsworth Jr. | Nixon | August 18, 1969 | Rejected (45-55) | November 21, 1969 |
| G. Harrold Carswell | Nixon | January 19, 1970 | Rejected (45-51) | April 8, 1970 |
| Robert H. Bork | Reagan | July 1, 1987 | Rejected (42-58) | October 23, 1987 |

[1.] Later nominated and confirmed.
[2.] Nominated for chief justice.
[3.] Later nominated for chief justice and confirmed.
Source: Library of Congress, Congressional Research Service.

Document Citation
Elder Witt & Joan Biskupic, Congressional

## An Unusual Insight Into Thomas Jefferson's Fear of the Federal Judiciary

"Though Jefferson accepted the Marbury decision, the Supreme Court still remained his favorite aversion. The position it attained as interpreter of the Constitution aroused his bitter antagonism. In the Supreme Court, he asserted, the Federal Party had entrenched itself for the purpose of destroying his Republican system. That had been his idea in 1801, when he ascended to power; that was his conviction in 1809, when Madison succeeded him in the Presidency; and that persuasion persisted for the seventeen years he lived in ostensible retirement. His last letters are full of such recriminations. The experiment in Republicanism had failed, largely because the judiciary was usurping the highest functions of government. 'The great object of my fear,' Jefferson wrote in 1821, 'is the Federal Judiciary. That body, like gravity, ever acting with noiseless foot, and unalarming advance, gaining ground step by step, and holding what it gains, is engulfing insidiously the special government into the jaws of that which feeds them.'
… 'It is a very dangerous doctrine to consider the judges as the ultimate arbiters of all constitutional questions. It is one which should place us under the despotism of an oligarchy….The Constitution has erected no such single tribunal.' And to Edward Livingston, a few months before Jefferson's death, the same foreboding was expressed: 'This member of the government [the Judiciary] was at first considered the most helpless and harmless of all its organs. But it has proved that its power of declaring what the law is, ad libitum, by sapping and mining, slyly, and without alarm, the foundations of the Constitution, could do what open force would not dare to attempt.'

"These are the words of a defeated man. And, so far as the Constitution was concerned, Jefferson had fought a losing battle. Many of the Jeffersonian ideas had passed into forgetfulness by the time of his death, and into the general discard had gone his belittlement of the judiciary."

—Burton J. Henrick, *Bulwark of the Republic: A Biography of the Constitution*. Boston: Little, Brown and Company, 1937, page 191

## A Very Small Bibliography to Introduce People to some Up-to-Date Neurological Thinking

Damasio, Antonio R., *Descartes' Error: Emotion, Reason, and the Human Brain.* New York: G.P.Putnam's Sons (A Grosset/Putnam Book), 1994.

Damasio, Antonio R., *The Feeling of What Happens: Body and Emotion in the Making of Consciousness.* San Diego: Harcourt,Inc. (A Harvest Book), 1999.

Damasio, Antonio R., *Looking for Spinoza: Joy, Sorrow, and the Feeling Brain.* New York: Harcourt, Inc., 2003.

Edelman, Gerald M., *The Remembered Present: A Biological Theory of Consciousness.* New York: Basic Books, 1989.

Edelman, Gerald M., *Bright Air, Brilliant Fire: On the Matter of the Mind.* New York: BasicBooks, 1992.

Edelman, Gerald M., *Wider Than the Sky: the Phenomenal Gift of Consciousness.* New Haven: Yale University Press, 2004

Edelman, Gerald M., and Tononi, Giulio, *A Universe of Consciousness: How Matter Becomes Imagination.* New York: BasicBooks, 1992.

Ledoux, Joseph, *The Emotional Brain: The Mysterious Underpinnings of Emotional Life.* New York: Simon & Schuster, 1996. LeDoux is referred to in Damasio, *Looking for Spinoza,* too.

Ledoux, Joseph, *Synaptic Self: How Our Brains Become Who We Are.* New York: Viking-Penguin, 2002.

Panksepp, Jaak "Feeling the Pain of Social Loss" Science, Vol.302 10 October, 2003 www.sciencemag.org
The author is at the J.P. Scott Center for Neuroscience, Mind Behavior, Dept of Psychology, Bowling Green State University, Bowling Green, OH 43403, and at the Falk Center for Molecular Therapeutics, Dept of Biomedical Engineering, Northwestern University, Evanston, IL 60201,

Panksepp, Jaak. *Affective Neuroscience: The Foundations of Human and Animal Emotions.* New York: Oxford University Press, 1998. Cited in Antonio Damasio, *Looking for Spinoza* on p.303 notes and p.307 notes.

Ridley, Matt, *Genome: The Autobiography of a Species in 23 Chapters,* HarperCollins, 1999.

Sapolsky, Robert, *Biology and Human Behavior: The Neurological Origins of Individuality*. Chantilly, VA 20151-1232: The Teaching Company (An audio book, Course No. 179 in the Great Courses Series.

Wordsworth, William, "Preface to Lyrical Ballads, Second Edition," 1800. This poet made the cut in our neuroscience bibliography because of his scrupulous discussion of the difference between his feelings about the ideas made from previous sense impressions and the feelings about the original sense impressions—a neat century and a half before most people knew enough to rejoice in that distinction. The "Preface.." nearly presages Gerald Edelman's comment, when writing about re-entry, that "the brain is more in touch with itself than with anything else." See also Wordsworth's famous and variously understood and misunderstood poem, "Ode: Intimations of Immortality from Recollections of Early Childhood".

\* The selections in this list by no means include all the writings by these authors. The list is a sampling for interested lay people.

# The Index

"Knights (The)," 21
"Managing Innovation When Less is More," 69n
"Politics and the English Language," 75
"The Home Front," 72
"The Inner Ring" 69
"The Ugly Duckling," 52
"Why I Write," 75
*A Terrible Love of War*, 15
*A Universe of Consciousness*, 35
Abstract language, 17, 29, 32
Administrator, administration, 17, 25, 26, 38
Aesop, 45
Alcibiades, 15, 16
Alcott, Bronson, 78
Altruism, 27, 47, 49, 57, 75, 76
American Academy of Pediatrics, 53n
American History, 12
Amnesty International, 67n
Andersen, Hans Christian, 51, 52
Aristophanes, 21
Athens, 15, 16
Auschwitz, 43
Balance of powers, 13
Bland language, 28, 33
Boethius, 17
Braun, Carol Mosley, 14
Bread for the World, 22n
*Bright Air, Brilliant Fire*, 35, 53n
Bryer, Stephen, 34n
Buddha, Buddhists, 22, 36, 66
Bully, bullying, 14, 16, 36, 43
Bush, George W., 13, 20, 22, 33n
Byrd, Senator Robert C., 11, 13, 14, 34, 79
Campaign for Innocent Victims in Conflict, 5
Capital Punishment, 34
*Carpet Boy's Gift*, 62
*Catcher in the Rye*, 66
Catholic Funds (the), 26n
*Changing the Bully Who Rules the World*, 28
Chaucer, G, 52
Children's Digital Media Centers, 53n
Christakis, Dimitri A., 53n
Christians, Christianity, 17, 22, 23, 26, 48
Church Folks for a Better America, 22n
Church of England, 19
Churchill, Winston, 11
Citigroup, 26n
Citygroup, 26
Civil Rights, 16
Clausewitz, Carl von, 14n, 68n, 76
Cleon, 21
Clergy and Laity Concerned About Iraq, 22n

Compassionate language, 18
Congress, 16, 33, 39
Consciousness, 33, 37, 45, 47, 49, 52ff, 56, 73
Constitution, 11, 12, 40
Cortex, neo-cortex, 27, 28, 29, 31, 38, 46, 48, 50, 56, 62, 64, 68, 74
Courage, 22, 36, 40
Cruel, cruelty, 10, 21, 22, 30, 35, 40, 47, 55, 69
Cultural relativism, 23
Damasio, Antonio, 27n, 53n, 62n
DiGiuseppe, David L., 53n
Dolan, John, 50n
Donne, John, 74
Dowd, Maureen, 22
*Down and Out in Paris and London*, 75
Dynamic, dynamics, 56-60, 76
Edelman, Gerald, 27n, 35, 53n
Eightfold Path, 36
Einstein, Albert, 64
Emerson, Ralph Waldo, 37, 41
Emery, Kathy, 32n, 54n
Empathy, empathic, 20, 30, 45 ff
Emperor, empire, 14, 16, 20, 30, 50
Evil, 13, 15, 19, 39, 48, 72
Executive Incentive Payment, 26n
*Feeling of What Happens (The)*, 27n, 53n, 62n
*Five Plays of Aristophanes*, 21n
Followers, 9, 18, 20, 22, 23, 33, 39, 41, 43
Forsheiser, Chris, 72
Freedom of Public Assemblage, 16
Freedom of Speech, 16
Freedom of the Press, 16
Gage, 60
Galatians, 18n
Galileo, 20
*Genocidal Mentality (The)*, 21n
George, Robert, 13
Ginsburg, Ruth Bader, 34n
Graves, Robert, 15
Greek, 15, 21, 50, 58
Grimm Brothers, 51
*Groupthink*, 24
*Guns of August (The)*, 15
Hale, Nathan, 19, 20, 26
Hardy, Thomas, 20
Harkness method, 17n
Harvard Divinity School, 37, 41
Harvard, 28, 41
Helms, Jesse, 14
Henry, Patrick, 26
Herbert, Bob, 22
Hillman, James, 15 (also in footnote)

Hitler, Adolf, 42, 43, 70
Holy language, 17, 28, 43
Homeland security, 22
Homeostasis, 31
Hope v. Pelzer, 33
House of Representatives, 11
Huckleberry Hound, 28
Imagining, imagination, 19, 26, 29, 45 ff
Industrial Psychology, 68n
IRS, 19
Ishiguro, Kazuo, 70
Ivan the Terrible, 43
James Madison Program in American Ideals and Institutions, 13n
Janis, Irving, 24
Jefferson, Thomas, 12, 40
Jesus, 19, 22, 26, 27, 29
John the Baptist, 15
Judicial, judiciary, 9, 11, 35, 39, 40
Judism, Jews, 17, 26, 43
Jungle philosophy, 46-53
Justice, 19, 20, 21, 30, 35, 36, 40, 48, 52, 62, 74, 78
Kaiser Family Foundation, 53n
Kennedy, Anthony M., 34
Kohlberg, Lawrence, 66, 75
Konopka, Gisela, 5
Leader, leadership, 9, 17, 18, 20, 25, 30, 33, 39, 72
Leadership Conference on Civil Rights, 33n
Lewis, C.S., 69, 70
Liberal Arts, 20, 23, 28
*Life*, 73
Lifton, Robert Jay, 21 (also in footnote)
Lincoln, Abraham, 13, 78
Losers, 40
Machiavelli, 14n, 68n
Management language, 18
Marbury v Madison, 12n, 89
Marcussen, Erik, 22n
Massachusetts Anti slavery Society, 16n
McCarty, Carolyn A. 53n
Mercy, merciful, 19, 30, 35, 40, 45, 52, 74, 78
Miller, Alice, 70
Milton, John, 48
Moral drift, 24, 25
Morris, William, 78
Moses, 22, 26, 29
Moyers, Bill, 22, 79
Napoleon, 43
National Council of Churches, 22n
National Foundation of Churches, 22n
National Mall, 9, 19, 41
Nazis, 22, 70
Nemeth, Charlan Jeanne, 69
Neurons, 45, 56, 73
Neuroscience, 27, 28, 38, 47, 49, 54, 60, 79
New Testament, 27

Ohanian, Susan, 32n, 54n
*Old Jules*, 28
Oliver, Mary, 17n
*On War*, 14n, 76
Orwell, George, 75, 79
Oxford, 28
Packer, George, 72
*Paradise Lost*, 48
Pathways, 58
Paulus, Field Marshal, 42, 43
Personal sacrifice, 29
Pharoah, 29
Phillips Exeter Academy, 17n
Phillips, Wendell, 16n
Porter, Katherine Ann, 13
Primary setting, 23
Princeton, 13n
Pryor, William, 33, 34
Psychological drift, 25,
Putterill, the Reverend Jack, 19
Rawls, John, 79
Re-entry, 16n, 27, 35, 73
*Remains of the Day*, 70
Republic, 16, 26, 39, 45, 50
Rice, Condoleezza, 15
Rights, 16
*Road to Wigan Pier (The)*, 75
Rogers, Carl, 75
Roper v Simmons, 34n
Ruskin, John, 78
Ruzicka, Marla, 5
Salinger, J.D., 66
Sandoz, Mari, 28
Sasson, Siegfried, 15
Schmooze language, 18, 43
Scorn, 40, 46, 64, 76
Secondary setting, 23, 27
Seinfeld, 28
Self-congratulation, 20
Senate, Senators 16, 18, 33, 34, 35, 39, 40,
Separation of Church and State, 16
Shea, Pegi Deitz, 62n
*Ship of Fools*, 13
Sicily, 16
Sisters of St. Joseph of Carondelet, 26n
Social Work, Social Worker, 23, 26, 32, 46, 47, 48, 49, 75E 2, 3
Socrates, 15, 49, 50, 52, 58, 64, 79
Solitude, 32
Solon, 58
Souter, David H., 34n
Spender, Stephen, 15
St. Paul, 18n
St. Philip of Heraklia, 17
Stage development philosophy, 20, 45 ff
Stanford, 28

Stevens, John Paul, 34n
Stone, I.F., 79
*Stopping the Gallop to Empire*, 77
Sun Tzu, 14n, 68n
Supreme Court, 11, 12, 16
*The New York Times*, 46
*The New Yorker*, 72
Theological concept, 48
Three Guineas, 72
*Three Readings for Republicans and Democrats*, 77
Trickery, 51
Tuchman, Barbara, 15
Twin Peaks, 28
United Daughters of the Confederacy, 14
Universal truths, 23, 49
University of California, Berkeley, 28
University of Minnesota Center for Youth Development, 5
Violence Against Women Act (US v. Morrison), 33
Virtue, 19, 29, 32, 45, 48, 58
Voting Rights Act, 33
Why is Corporate America Bashing Our Public Schools?, 32n, 54n
Woolf, Virginia, 72, 73, 79
Wordsworth, William, 17n, 27n
Yale, 15n
Zimmerman, Frederick J., 53n

Carol Bly's most recent books are *Beyond the Writers' Workshop* (Anchor Books, 2001), and *Changing the Bully Who Rules the World* (Milkweed, 1996. 3rd printing, 2005). Three chapters of her as of now unpublished novel, *Shelter Half*, have appeared in *The Idaho Review* and *Prairie Schooner.*

She was a June, 2005, visiting writing instructor in Hofsos, Iceland, and at Indiana University. She is teaching The Short Story in the Hamline University graduate writing program, Fall, 2005, and will be a visiting instructor in the University of Nebraska's Writers' Conference, June, 2006.

She and Cynthia Loveland together have published two previous books with Bly & Loveland Press: *Three Readings for Republicans and Democrats* and *Stopping the Gallop to Empire.*

Cynthia Loveland is recently retired from her career as a Social Worker. After earning her MSW at the University of Minnesota she worked for nine years in county social service in rural Minnesota. She then worked for almost 30 years as a School Social Worker for the St. Paul Public Schools.

She has been active in professional and community organizations—including a two term stint as Secretary of the Board of the Minnesota Chapter of the National Association of Social Workers (NASW) and as Chair of the Pamphlet Committee of the Minnesota School Social Workers' Association (MSSWA).

Carol Bly and Cynthia Loveland